Acupoint Magnet Therapy

"Magnet Acupuncture"

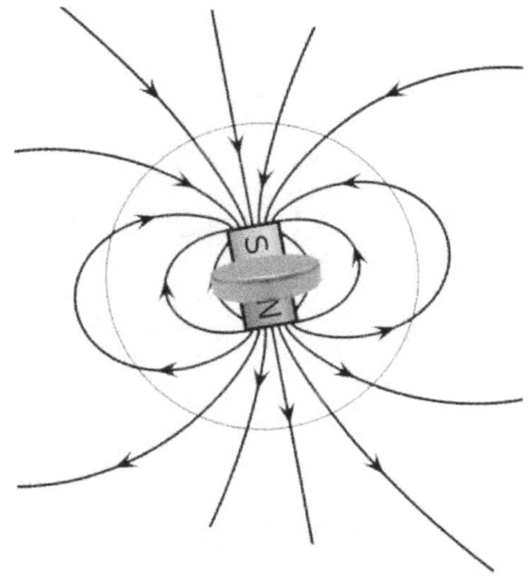

Nam Jeon, L.Ac.　全湳旭

8/15/2019

Acupoint Magnet Therapy

ISBN: 9781696591553

+

BISAC: Medicine/General
HEA032000
Published and distributed by Nam W. Jeon
Printed in the United States of America by KDP

DEDICATION

"I dedicate this work to the loving memory of my son, Kana Jeon."

Preface

Acupuncture has been used for thousands years to treat pain and functional disorders. However, there are cost and time restraints for people to receive acupuncture treatment. There is a simple self-help to relieve minor ache and pain, or life limiting symptoms using magnets.

My other book "Meridian Therapy Handbook" explains in depth theory of Traditional Chinese Medicine and the practical reference guide to treat many disorders. However, in this book "Acupoint Magnet Therapy" I summarized the section of the magnetic therapy part available to use for everybody.

This book will provide readers with a quick and ready to use information on how to treat many disorders with magnets put on acupuncture points.

DISCLAIMER

Information in this book is for educational purposes only. It is not intended to treat any undiagnosed disorders. If you have any health concerns, first you need to see a licensed health care provider.

Acupoint Magnet Therapy

Introduction

Chapter 1: Theory of MAGNETIC THERAPY

Magnet therapy alternative to acupuncture needle, is explained. An easy and simple way of alleviating disorders by magnet and magnetic Ring is introduced.

Chapter 2: Acupoint Treatment with Magnet

Acupuncture points for treating chronic pain is introduced, body including acupuncture points and ear acupuncture points

Chapter 3: The Twelve Principal Meridians
Physiological functions of twelve meridians and indications of when they are out of balance, is explained. Treatment protocol table of the Five phases Acupuncture (Sa Ahm Acupuncture) and Yuan Source Points are introduced.

Chapter 4: About the pain
The types of pain, pain medications, and mindful meditation as pain management tool are explained.

Chapter 5: Acupuncture Point Location

ACUPUNCTURE POINT LOCATION PICTURES ARE SHOWN FOR EASY REFERENCE.

Nam W Jeon, L. Ac.

Acupoint Magnet Therapy

CONTENTS

CHAPTER: 1
Magnetic Therapy

CHAPTER: 2
Magnetic Treatment on Acupoint

CHAPTER: 3
Meridians

CHAPTER: 4

All about the pain

CHAPTER: 5

PICTURES: ACUPUNCTURE POINT LOCATION

CHAPTER: 6

Acupoint Magnet Therapy

"Magnet Acupuncture"

CHAPTER ONE

1-1. Magnetic Therapy

Acupuncture & Magnetic Field Therapy
Excerpt from the article in Acupuncture Today August 2019   By William Pawluk, MD, MSc

William Pawluk is an assistant professor at Johns Hopkins Medical School. He has published a book, "Magnetic Therapy in Eastern Europe: a Review of 30 years of Research."

Magnets stimulate acupuncture points and meridians. Although this use is not prominent in the West, it is utilized in China, Japan and Korea as an alternative to needles. In 1990, when I began treating people with acupuncture, they did not necessarily resist the idea of acupuncture but did balk at the needles. Therefore, I began to look at alternative approaches to doing acupuncture. That is when I discovered that magnets were used on acupuncture points in China, Japan and Korea—an example is Koryo Hand Therapy.1

In recent years our understanding of how and why they can work has been expanded to not only magnets, but also to a much wider potential value by the use of pulsed electromagnetic fields (PEMFs). Therefore, the use of magnetic stimulation in acupuncture can lead to significantly enhanced effectiveness of acupuncture in general.

Early Experiences With Magnets

One of my earliest cases using magnets involved a friend of the family who used to have motion sickness. I used a high intensity quarter inch wide magnet taped superficially without any pressure to Nei Guan (P6) bilaterally. He went for a ride in his car and returned delighted that he did not get nauseous and dizzy. Because they worked so well with him, I had a puppy that got carsick and would vomit as well. I fashioned similar magnets over the same point on the dog's forelimbs. We had the same experience with the dog, which was able to move around on the backseat of the car without any evidence of dizziness. We used the magnets on the dog every time we went in the car with equal success.

Another patient was complaining of dental jaw pain, so I applied similar small magnets without pressure over the Hegu (LI4) point bilaterally. Within minutes the pain in the jaw disappeared. Another patient had what appeared to be tension headaches and magnets were taped to a headband and placed over GB20 (Feng Chi) points bilaterally, not even touching the skin. It only took minutes for the pain to decrease by over 50 percent.

I expanded my use of magnets beyond acupuncture points and further discovered that magnets had many actions on tissues directly and provided pain relief that did not rely on acupuncture principles specifically. They didn't even need to be applied on "ah shi" spots, but could in fact be used for all sorts of superficial tissue problems including insect bites, bruises, sprains and strains, cuts and abrasions, even surgical wounds. The results were often dramatic. One time I put a two-inch diameter, flat disk magnet on a large, deep purple thigh bruise in the evening. In the morning the woman noticed a completely clear area in the center of the bruise, where the magnet was placed.

When I worked with nurses, many complained of menstrual migraines. I thought, why not use magnetic necklaces to help with the migraines or even to prevent them. Magnetic necklaces affect all the meridians passing through the neck. Many nurses adopted this magnetic necklace therapy and would start wearing the necklaces about 3 to 4 days premenstrually.

I was very intrigued with magnets and what they were doing. I scoured the scientific literature on how magnets work physiologically. Much of the science was in foreign languages, especially Eastern European. Along the way a doctor from the Czech Republic, who had translated a lot of this Eastern European research, shared a manuscript. As a result we collaborated on the publication of the book, "Magnetic Field Therapy in Eastern Europe: a review of 30 years of research." 2

How PEMFs Differ From Acupuncture
What is PEMF Therapy? PEMF stands for Pulsed Electromagnetic Field. Devices that utilize PEMF technology emit electromagnetic waves at different wavelengths in order to stimulate and encourage your body's natural recovery process.

While this journey started with the frustration of people not being willing to have acupuncture, it led to the discovery of the extensive value of magnetic fields in not only stimulating acupuncture points and meridians but also the value of treating diseased and damaged tissue in ways that acupuncture can't. In other words, acupuncture works mostly through indirect stimulation of the bodies systems while magnets and PEMFs can do both indirect as well as direct therapy. Therefore, combining the use of acupuncture and magnetic field/PEMF therapy makes a lot of sense to significantly enhance the benefits of acupuncture.

What makes the approach of combining acupuncture and PEMFs synergistic has a basis in science. PEMFs affect acupuncture points and meridians because evidence shows that the points and meridians are an electrical system. Dr. Robert Becker, author of "The Body Electric"3 discovered this in his lab. Acupuncture points and meridians were a direct current (DC) system and that acupuncture points had increased electrical conductivity.4

Dr. Kaung-Ti Yung, from the Department of Physics, at Geneva College, Penn., wrote a series of articles, "A Birdcage Model for the Chinese Meridian System." The first one was: Part I. A Channel as a Transmission Line.5 He describes how this is possible from an engineering and physics perspective. In other words, there is a constant flow of a low level, approximately 10-microampere current throughout the whole system around-the-clock.

These findings are important because of a law of physics, Faraday's law; a magnetic field will interact with an electric circuit to produce an electromotive force (EMF) - a phenomenon called electromagnetic induction. Electromagnetic induction in the tissues of the body results in the production of charge (energy) in the tissues. In other words, the flow of natural charge in the tissues and the presence of the movement of charged ions, interacting with a magnetic field, whether static or pulsed, will result in increased charge in the tissues. Since acupuncture points and meridians have physical aspects of an electrical system, PEMFs interacting with them will result in increased charge and energy in the body and hence increased benefits and results.

Electro-acupuncture is an acknowledgement that the acupuncture system is electrical. Electro-stimulation of points ends up stimulating and increasing the amount of electrical charge coursing through the meridians. It is well established that electro acupuncture stimulation is very dynamic and produces similar, and in many cases better, benefits to regular, manual needle acupuncture. Electromagnetic stimulation of points is essentially the same, but without the electrical charge being introduced into the body. Rather, electromagnetic stimulation causes the body to produce its own charge through the interaction of the magnetic fields with charge, and ions carrying charge, already present in the body.

How PEMFs Work

PEMF or electro-magnetic stimulation can be used before, during or after manual needle acupuncture. In fact, PEMF therapy can be used in other parts of the body from where acupuncture is being applied. The main value of PEMF therapy is deep, direct tissue penetration. It can be used to assist acupuncture for stubborn-to-manage problems where the tissues need to be stimulated directly for direct tissue healing. This is especially true for the direct healing of organs, such as the lungs, heart, liver, kidneys, etc. Functional problems can be helped significantly with acupuncture, possibly even more than with PEMFs. Therefore, combining PEMFs and acupuncture would be more helpful for both the functional and the tissue healing aspects of health problems.

There is a large amount of scientific evidence for the clinical use of PEMFs as a sole modality and is reviewed extensively in the book Power Tools for Health: how magnetic fields [PEMFs] help you.6

PEMFs in My Practice

I use PEMFs to heal almost any tissue. The most common use of PEMFs is to help with pain, especially with arthritis. The main difference between using PEMFs for pain and acupuncture is that PEMFs have the direct issue action of reducing inflammation and edema, improving circulation and a natural pain killing effect, locally. In other words, PEMFs help to heal the cause of the pain not just with pain reduction. Because they improve circulation, they can be dramatically helpful in healing circulatory ulcers and wounds.

A specific example is a 50-year-old man who had bilateral diabetic gangrene from the knees down. He was recommended bilateral below knee amputations. He was started on an appropriate diet, supplements, and PEMF therapy. With aggressive therapy, several hours a day in the home setting, and very close clinical follow-up, he had relatively rapid progressive improvement in circulation. In three months, his surgeon declared that he did not really need amputations anymore.

Everyone knows there are no effective brain treatments for concussion, with people healing essentially on their own and only receiving symptomatic management. Ten people were treated following mild to moderate concussions with a portable PEMF system, for two hours per day over three months. They were regularly monitored with an objective sensory cortical test device. They all showed improvement after one or two weeks in symptoms, test scores and cognitive function. This benefit was maintained for at least three months.

Evidence in Combining PEMFs With Acupuncture

One study compared PEMF stimulation of BL15 with manual acupuncture and laser acupuncture. The three methods of stimulation were evaluated for their effects on the autonomic nervous system, using heart rate variability measurements. Manual acupuncture and PEMF stimulation activated the parasympathetic nervous system almost equally whereas laser acupuncture activated the sympathetic nervous system. This means that manual acupuncture and PEMFs induced better relaxation in the body.7

Application of magnetic fields to acupuncture points have also been found helpful in number of conditions: PC6 (Neiguan) stimulation has been found to balance the autonomic nervous system (ANS),8 help with plantar fasciitis9 and stroke,10 reduce pain in infants,11 reduce chronic low back pain,12 improve recovery of the quadriceps muscle from muscle fatigue following exercise13 and in the treatment of temporomandibular joint [TMJ] disorders.14 The value of using physical magnets on acupuncture points has been reviewed,15 lending further support to combining these modalities.

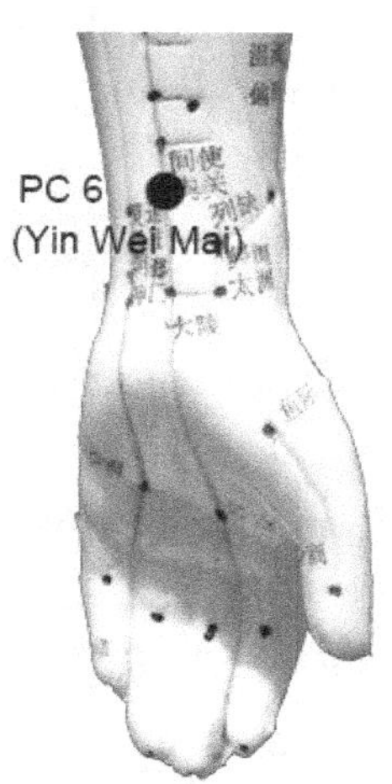

Another recent study looked at using high intensity PEMFs to stimulate PC6 (Neiguan) and its effect on the brain EEG. The PEMF at PC6 induced a powerful brain response, enhancing brain plasticity, which is helpful for neurotrauma, stroke, infections and many other neurological problems.16 Treatment of patients with combined anxiety and depression (CAD) using electro acupuncture to multiple points and high intensity PEMFs to the brain works better with the combination than the standard medical therapy using PEMFs alone.17

Why is it important for acupuncturists to know about the use of magnetic fields in their acupuncture practices? All clinicians see patients who either do not respond at all or do not respond adequately to their usual tools. This is true for all health care professions. Also, patients often present with multiple problems, requiring multiple modalities to get the best results. Some of these problems are more responsive to acupuncture than others. Once a relationship is established with the patient, it would be helpful to both the acupuncturist and the patient to be able to solve as many of the patients' problems as possible without the need for referrals to other practitioners, medical or otherwise.

In highly competitive professional environments, the more options a practitioner can offer patients, the more successful the practice. One of the professional disciplines most competitive with acupuncturists is chiropractors. Both professions see mostly patients with musculoskeletal and pain problems. Chiropractors have increasingly embraced and integrated PEMF therapy into their practices, increasing the competition with acupuncturists. Because it is fairly clear that PEMF therapy integrated with acupuncture, produces better results and significantly extends the benefits of treatments and the numbers and types of patients that can be seen, acupuncturists need to learn more about PEMF therapies and how they can be integrated into their practices.

1-2. Theory: MAGNET THERAPY

Magnet therapy uses static magnetic fields produced by permanent magnets.
Since well-designed, placebo-controlled studies of magnet therapy have been rare, it is difficult to verify the effectiveness of magnetic therapy. One such well-publicized study at Baylor College of Medicine in Houston suggested that magnet therapy significantly reduced knee pain in 50 patients with post-polio syndrome, although even those who received sham therapy also reported some improvement. Another placebo-controlled study by a plastic surgeon in Boca Raton, Fla., indicated that magnet therapy could significantly reduce the pain and swelling that typically follows liposuction. Other studies found magnets helped control foot pain in people with diabetes as well as the pain of dental extractions. Magnet therapy has also helped promote the healing of fractures that fail to unite.

The position of the National Center for Complementary and Integrative Health (NCCIH) on magnet therapy is in the NCCIH's website states, "Scientific evidence does not support the use of magnets for pain relief."

Research studies do not support the use of static magnets for any form of pain.
Electromagnets may help with osteoarthritis, but it is unclear if they can relieve the pain enough to improve quality of life and day-to-day functioning, a 2013 research review concluded. For osteoarthritis, small machines or mats are used to deliver electromagnetic fields to the whole body or to certain joints.
In 2013 the U.S. Food and Drug Administration approved a device that uses strong electromagnets to treat migraines by stimulating nerve cells in the brain, a process called transcranial magnetic stimulation (TMS). TMS may help other pain conditions as well.

Safety

Acupoint Magnet Therapy

Some magnets may interfere with medical devices, such as pacemakers and insulin pumps.
Beyond interference with medical devices, there is not much good information on the possible side effects of magnets, but few problems have been reported.
Children may swallow or accidentally inhale small magnets, which can be deadly.
Do not use static magnets or electromagnets that you can buy without a prescription, to postpone seeing a health care provider about pain or any other medical problem

Despite a lack of scientific evidence to support claims that commercially available magnetic therapy devices work, wearable magnets remain extremely popular. Global sale of therapeutic magnets is estimated to be at least $1 billion a year, according to the BBC.

1-3. Meridian Therapy with Magnet

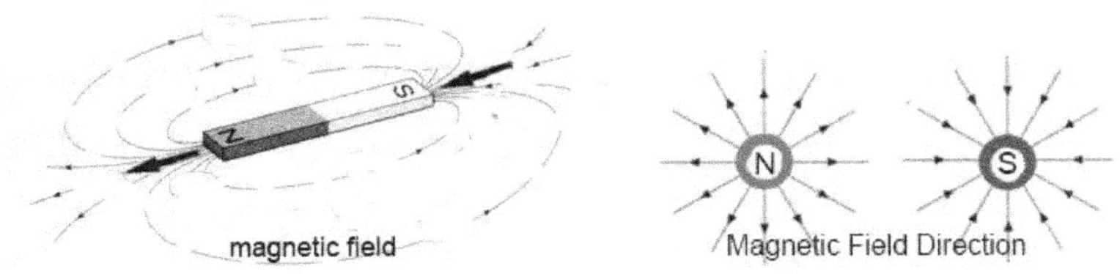

The north pole of a magnet is defined as the pole that points towards the Earth's North Magnetic Pole in the Arctic. Since opposite poles attract, the North Magnetic Pole is actually the south pole of the Earth's magnetic field.

The flow direction of the magnetic field is from the north to the south pole of the magnet. Which means that the north pole of a magnet has dispersing energy and the south pole of a magnet has collecting energy. This property is used to replace acupuncture needles in meridian magnet therapy.

A magnet with the power of 500 - 3000 gauss is used to replace the acupuncture needle to stimulate acupuncture points. Applying the north pole side of a magnet on an acupuncture point can trigger pushing (tonifying) effect, while applying the south pole can trigger absorbing (sedation) effect. The north pole will stimulate, while the South pole will sedate or calm the meridian.

Here is one clinical trial done in Kyonggi University, South Korea in Feb. 11, 2008 – Aug. 29/2008. An Effect of Magnetic Therapy applying the Principal of Sa-am Acupuncture on Menstrual Pain and Distress of Female High School Students.

By Kim, Ji Min (사암침 원리를 적용한 자기요법이 여고생 월경통 및 월경전후 증상에 미치는 효과)

Experimental Group: 30
Control Group: 30
Magnet used: N.D (Neodymium), 5 mm Diameter, 1.5 mm thickness, 2600 Gauss

Sa Ahm Acupuncture protocol: Small Intestine Tonification.
Tonification: SI 3, GB 41, N pole to face acupuncture point
Sedation: SI 2, BL66, S pole to face acupuncture point

Treatment is done for 3 days before the onset of menstruation.

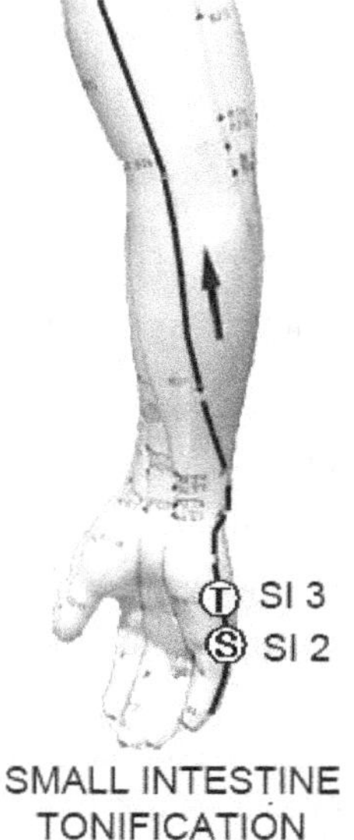

SMALL INTESTINE
TONIFICATION

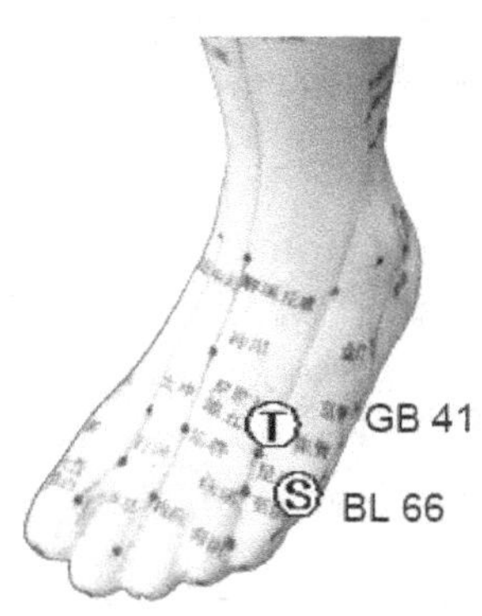

The summary of the results of the research would be as follows.

1. The experimental group undergoing magnetic therapy had less intensity of menstrual pain than the control group. (F=44.798,p<0.001).
2. The experimental group undergoing magnetic therapy had taken less menstrual pain reliever during the menstruation period than that of the control group.(F=44.798,p<0.001).
3. The experimental group undergoing magnetic therapy experienced reduced menstrual pain duration the menstruation period than the control group. (F=53.541,p<0.001).
4. The experimental group undergoing the magnetic therapy had statistically relevant results for the reduced menstrual distress such as abdominal pain, waist pain, pain spreading to thigh, breast tenderness, perineal and anal pain, flank pain, headache, vaginal discharge and leukorrhea, dizziness, digestive disorder, diarrhea, , decreased mental concentration, nervousness and depression than the control group's distress.
5. Finally, compared to the control group, the experimental group undergoing magnetic therapy had shown no statistically relevant difference in terms of menstrual distress, such as nausea/vomiting, improving/decreasing appetite, constipation, edema, insomnia and anxiety.

In conclusion, the researcher recommends magnetic therapy, applying the principle of Sa Ahm Acupuncture to be used for relieving menstrual pain. This remedy has been effective in improving menstruation distress, and the reduction of menstrual pain reliever simultaneously.

1-4. Magnets to use

Magnet A: This strong, gold plated disc magnet is a great choice for magnetic therapy applications on the body. Dimensions: 1/4 " dia x 1/16" thick (6 mm x 1.6 mm)
Material: NdFeB, Grade N52
Plating/Coating: Ni-Cu-Ni-Au (Gold)
Surface Field: 3309 Gauss

Magnet B: This small, nickel plated disc magnet is a great choice for magnetic therapy applications on the hand, foot and ear.

Dimensions: 3mm dia. x 1.5mm thick
Material: NdFeB, Grade N35
Plating/Coating: Ni-Cu-Ni (Nickel)
Surface Field: 4278 Gauss

Magnet C: This little magnet is coated with a durable layer of two-tone plastic. This dual-color plastic coating is designed to make it easy to identify the poles. The red half is the North side of the magnet. The black half is the South side of the magnet. Use them to identify the poles of another magnet..

Dimensions: 3/8" dia. x 1/2" thick
Material: NdFeB, Grade N42
Plating/Coating: Ni-Cu-Ni-Plastic
Surface Field: 5023 Gauss

Magnet Set: It comes with 10 of magnet A, 5 of magnet B, and one of Magnet C in a plastic carrying case.

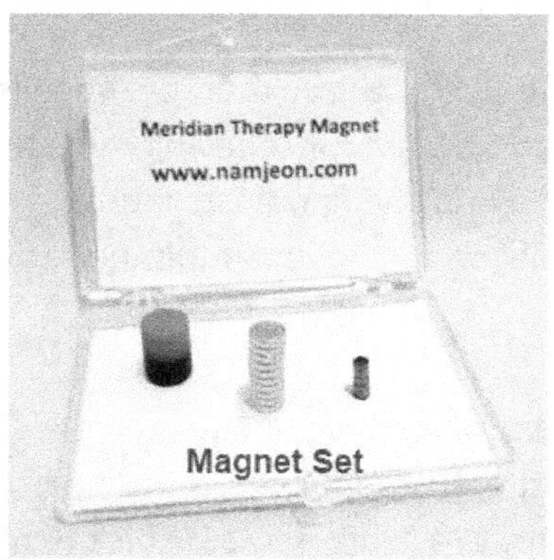

1-5. Tape

Acupoint Magnet Therapy

3M 1527-1 Transpore Surgical Tape 1" x 10 Yard.

This tape is highly recommended, because it does not cause a skin allergy reaction with long-term use, and is water resistant.
Transparent, water-resistant, perforated plastic tape, with easy bi-directional tears, hypoallergenic and Latex-free.

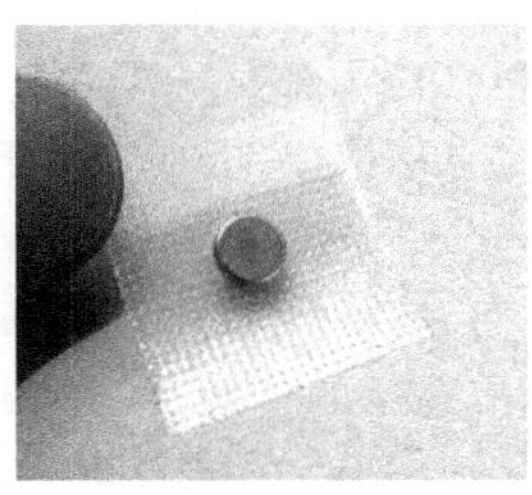

Cut the tape about 1" x 1" square, and place the magnet in the center. Make sure the desired pole (N or S pole) faces the acupuncture point.

For a small magnet, cut the tape ½" x ½" size. Tape can be cut bi-directionally easily with fingers.

Place the tape with magnet firmly on the acupuncture point.

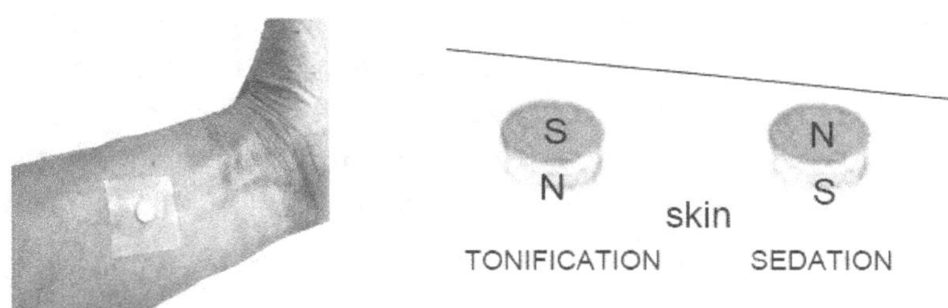

1-5. About Magnet Therapy.

1. Does polarity really matter?

Some practitioners do not believe that the polarity matters after the trial without polarity consideration. Acupuncture points have the natural capability of self-regulating homeostatic balance when the external energy is applied.

Since in the practice of Sa Ahm Acupuncture Meridian Therapy, tonification and sedation are the most important concepts, I prefer to consider the polarity for treatment. However, if you treat pain, select the polarity that works the best after a few trials reversing polarity. N pole is for tonifying, and S pole is for sedation.

2.   Which side should I put the magnet on?

If you treat pain, normally select the acupuncture points on the painful side of the body. If it does not help, try the same points on the opposite side of the body. Sometimes treating the non-painful side works as well. If you treat the functional disorder with multiple points on the upper and lower limbs, select one point on either side of the upper limb. A second point can be selected on the contralateral side, or the same (ipsilateral) side of the lower limb. For example, if one point on the right arm/hand is selected, a second point can be selected on either the right or the left leg.

3.   How long should I leave the magnet on?

There is no magic formula for the duration of time to get the results. Sometimes pain gets better within a few days, sometimes it may take a few weeks to see the result. Applying a magnet on the same spot on the body more than three days is not recommended, as it may cause skin irritation. If treatment takes longer than three days, you need to remove the magnet for a day, or put the magnet on the opposite side of the body. Acupuncture points are bilaterally located on the right and the left side of the body.

Pain treatment: Leave the magnet on the selected acupuncture point for two or three days. Give a day of rest, and put the magnet on to avoid skin irritation. Repeat the cycle until the problem is resolved. If you do not see results, try it with the reversed polarity. If you tried treatment with the N pole touching the acupuncture point, next time try it with the S pole touching the skin.

Functional Treatment: Apply the magnet on the selected acupuncture point for two or three days. Change the treatment point to the opposite side of the body. Repeat the cycle until the problem is resolved. You may experience a slow the improvement of the symptoms, but functional disorder treatment may take 2 – 3 months to see results.

If you experience any kind of side effect such as nausea, vomiting, headache, insomnia, pain, high blood pressure, or palpitation, take the magnet off immediately. Magnet therapy may not work for you.

1-6. Meridian Magnetic Ring

The 12 regular meridian pathways either start or end in the fingers and toes. In the fingers and toes a few of the Five Shu points are located, which strongly influence the meridian energetic. The idea of the therapeutic magnetic ring is because the magnetic force can influence the meridian energy flow. The polarity of the magnet creates the magnetic field from the N pole to the S pole. Consequently, by aligning the magnetic field direction to the meridian flow direction, the meridian energy can be strengthened (Tonification). Conversely, by aligning in the opposite direction, the meridian energy can be weakened (Sedation).

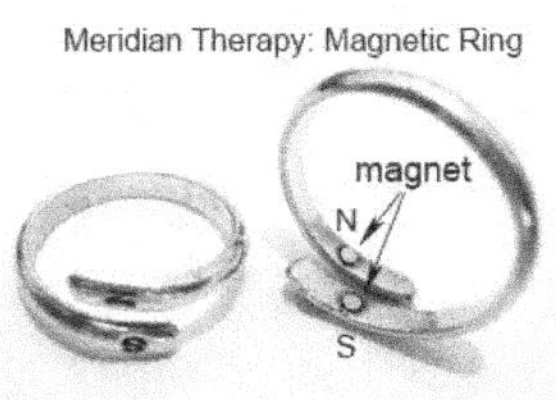

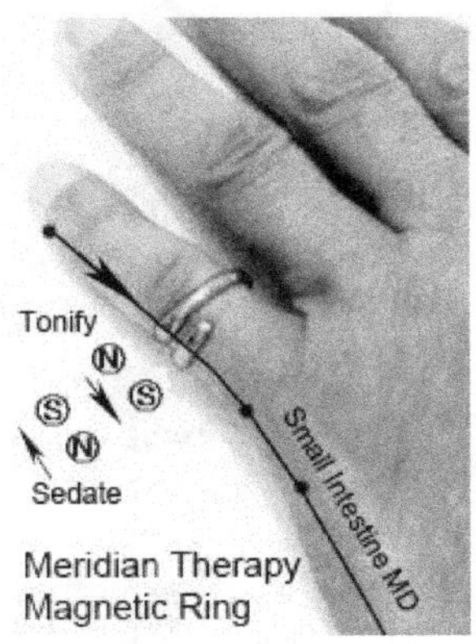

In theory, the 12 regular meridians, except the Kidney meridian, which does not originate from any toe, can be tonified or sedated with this method.

Tonification and sedation applied to the thumb (the Lung Meridian) and the index finger (the Large Intestine Meridian), helped with the seasonal allergy symptoms. The Lung and the Large Intestine meridians are the paired meridians with the metal element that are responsible for the respiratory functions and respiratory allergy.

Tonification and sedation applied to the second toe (the Stomach Meridian) and the big toe (the Spleen Meridian), may help with weight loss. The Spleen and the Stomach meridians are the paired meridians with the earth element that are responsible for the digestive function.

Acupoint Magnet Therapy

Refer to CHAPTER 10, MERIDIAN TONIFICATION AND SEDATION, to identify the meridian that is responsible for the symptoms you want to treat. Also keep in mind that the paired Yin and Yang meridians can be used alternatively, reversing the Tonification and Sedation method. For example, instead of the Lung Tonification, the Large Intestine Sedation method can be used.

Once the meridian is selected, refer to the following pictures to identify the meridian and the flow direction.

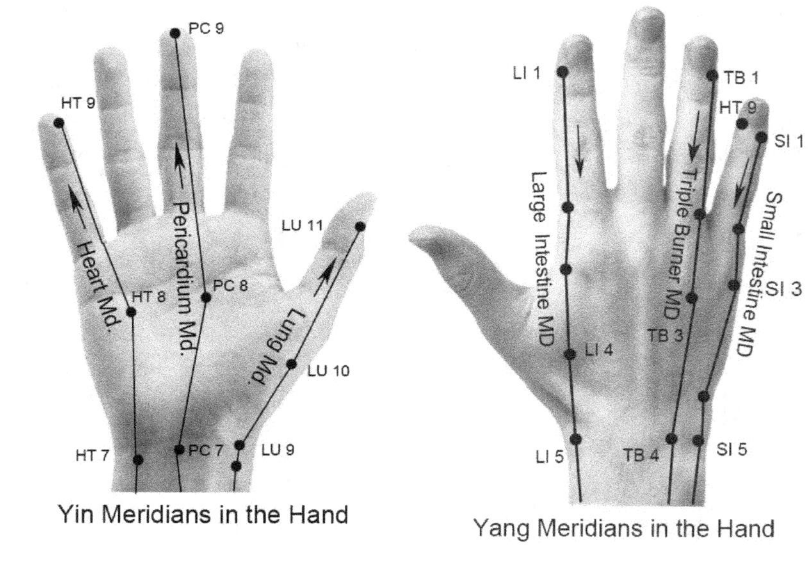

Yin Meridians in the Hand   Yang Meridians in the Hand

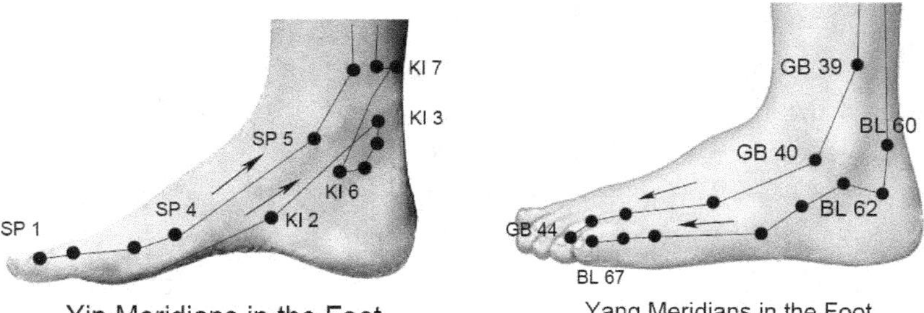

Yin Meridians in the Foot   Yang Meridians in the Foot

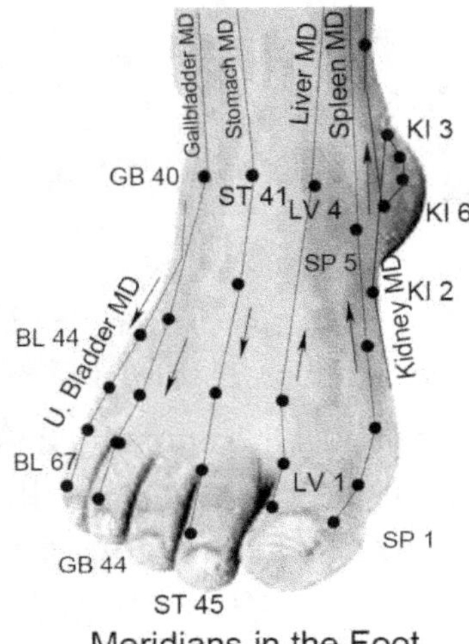

Meridians in the Foot

Meridian Legend
SP: Spleen, ST: Stomach, GB: Gallbladder, BL: Urinary bladder, KI: Kidney, LV: Liver, LI: Large intestine, LU: Lung, HT: Heart, PC: Pericardium, TB: Triple burner, SI: Small intestine

CHAPTER TWO

2-1. Acupoint Treatment with Magnet

2-1-1. Acupuncture Points

Acupuncture points are mostly located on 14 major meridians, pathways which run throughout the body and according to Traditional Chinese Medicine (TCM) transport life energy (Qi, 氣). Twelve of these major meridians, commonly referred to as "the primary meridians," are bilateral and are associated with internal organs. There are also points that are not located on the fourteen major meridians, and they are often referred to as "extra points."
In practice, an anatomical landmarks, palpation, and feedback from the patient locate acupuncture points.
In the following chapter, meridians and acupuncture points for treating disorders are illustrated. If you find the point location is not clear, you can find the more detail of point location in the internet, Google and YouTube.

Ashi point

An Ashi point (阿是穴) is an area where a person perceives pain or discomfort in the body. An Ashi point and the actual problem area may not be the same. An Ashi point can be created by physical trauma, or it can be created without an individual knowing it, by over-straining a specific muscle or tendon. An Ashi point is also known as a trigger point.

In TCM, treating the perceived location of discomfort or pain without addressing its underlying causes, is regarded as a branch treatment. On the other hand, fixing the root cause of the problem is called a root treatment. Ashi point treatment is a more practical first line of treatment for musculoskeletal pain.

Most often, where a person feels pain is not necessarily the actual cause of that pain. If a person has a painful back, that pain might be coming from an injury or blockage somewhere along the pathway of the meridian (Musculo-Tendinous Meridian 筋經 Jin Jing).

Despite the widespread use of Ashi point treatment (or trigger point therapy) in western medicine, the application of Ashi point treatment as a cohesive treatment is limited. The root treatment has to be incorporated to resolve the problem from the source. This is why TCM meridian therapy is more comprehensive and effective in treating pain than any other treatment technique.

2-1-2. Procedure: Pain Treatment

1. Find the Ashi point
    If the Ashi point is not obvious, palpate the problem area and find the "OUCHIE!" spot (阿是穴 Ashi point) - the most reactive, tender, sore, or painful spot
2. Find pain source point if it can be located.
    The source point can be where the muscle spasm or node is present in the muscle or tendon area near the Ashi point.
3. Select a couple of acupuncture points nearest to the Ashi or Source point in reference to the acupuncture point location charts.
4. Treat all selected points - Sedation for acute pain, or Tonification for chronic pain. Some acupuncturists claim that the needling technique of tonification and sedation is not important. The body has a self-healing mechanism and is able to use stimulation by the acupuncture needle to its benefit even though the practitioner may not perform the tonification and sedation technique.

2-2. Chronic Pain

Symptoms:

Chronic pain is often defined as any pain lasting more than 12 weeks. Whereas acute pain is a normal sensation that alerts us to possible injury. Chronic pain is very different. Chronic pain persists, often for months or even longer.

Acupoint Magnet Therapy

Chronic pain may arise from an initial injury, such as a back sprain, or there may be an ongoing cause, such as illness. However, there may also be no clear cause. Other health problems, such as fatigue, sleep disturbance, decreased appetite, and mood changes, often accompany chronic pain. Chronic pain may limit a person's movement, which can reduce flexibility, strength, and stamina. This can lead to disability and despair.

Diagnosis:

Pain is a very personal and subjective experience. There is no test that can measure and locate pain with precision. Therefore, health professionals rely on the patient's own description of the type, timing, and location of pain. Defining pain as sharp or dull, constant or intermittent, or burning or aching may give the best clues to the cause of the pain.

Cause:

When injury or inflammation occurs, cells at the site of pain release a variety of biochemical mediators. These mediators, such as prostaglandins, cytokines, chemokines, and growth factors, bind to, and activate sensory nerves in the periphery.

Signals are transmitted from the peripheral nervous system (PNS) to the central nervous system (CNS). When the pain is acute, signaling typically stops once the cause of pain is resolved. When pain is chronic, the signal persists over time, and can lead to biochemical changes in the nervous system. Several neuro mediators have been identified as drivers of chronic pain.

Peripheral Sensitization: Increases in the levels of mediators causes a persistent increase in the number of pain signals transmitted through the PNS, a state known as peripheral sensitization

Central Sensitization: Peripheral sensitization may lead to central sensitization, which can exacerbate chronic pain. In central sensitization, the chemistry of sensory neurons in the CNS is altered, changing how signals are processed. As a result, the CNS remains in a persistent state of high reactivity, resulting in a heightened perception of pain.

To treat chronic pain caused by Central Sensitization in the brain the focus has to be on the brain rather than to the perceived site of pain.

Treatment

If chronic pain cannot be cured, it can be managed. The following treatments are among the most common ways to manage pain. Medications, acupuncture, electrical stimulation, nerve blocks, or surgery are some treatments used for chronic pain. Psychotherapy, meditation, biofeedback, tai chi, massage therapy and behavior modification may also be used to treat chronic pain. Many people find complementary or alternative medicine approaches can provide additional relief.

2-2-1. How to treat chronic pain

All chronic illnesses and disabilities involve some disorder in the human spirit including emotional disorders or mental stress.

Acupuncture has long been used for emotional, psychological and spiritual disorders in the east. Qi is the life force that regulates spiritual, emotional, and physical balance. Thus, promoting an energetic balance of Qi in the body results in the harmonization of mind, body, and spirit.

Increasing evidence supports a biological basis for the use of acupuncture to treat mental health conditions. In the treatment of depression, acupuncture stimulates the nerve fibers that transmit impulses to various parts of the central nervous system and induce the release of serotonin, norepinephrine, substance P, dopamine, b-endorphin, and dynnorphins, primarily in the hypothalamus.

In addition to Meridian Therapy pain treatment protocol, you may add one or two of the following acupuncture points for mental and emotional stress to calm the spirit.

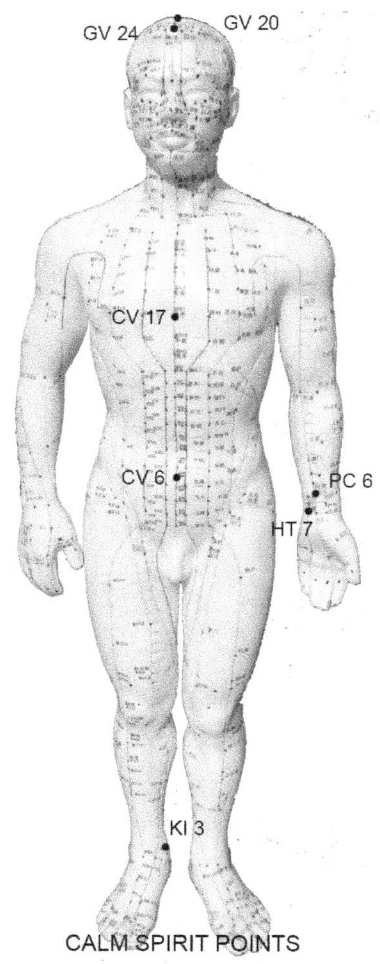

Calming Spirit Acupuncture Points: PC 6, HT 7, GV 20, CV 17, CV 6.

Ear Acupuncture Points to relieve pain: Shen Men, Thalamus, Cingulate Gyrus.

[POINT LOCATION]

GV20 (Baihui): Crossing point of two lines, 7 cun above the midpoint of the posterior hairline (5 cun above midpoint of anterior hairline), and midway on a line connecting the apex of both ears.

GV24 (Shenting): 0.5 cun above the midpoint of the anterior hairline.

CV 17 (Shanzhong): On the midline level with the 4th intercostal space midway between the nipples.

CV6 (Qihai): On the midline, 1.5 cun inferior to the umbilicus.

PC6 (Neiguan): 2 cun above the transverse crease of the wrist PC7, between palmaris longus and flexor carpi radialis tendons, on the line

HT7 (Shenmen): On the ulnar end of the transverse crease of the wrist, in the small depression between the pisiform and ulna bones.

2-3. Auricular (Ear) Acupuncture

Ear acupuncture has been used for addiction recovery and PTSD treatment. The auricular area of the ear has many powerful reflex points that can stimulate certain parts of the brain.

Acupoint Magnet Therapy

Ear Tack (Press Needle), Ear Pellet (Ear Seed), or Small Magnet can be placed in the ear acupuncture points.

Ear Pellet

Ear Tack
(Press Needle)

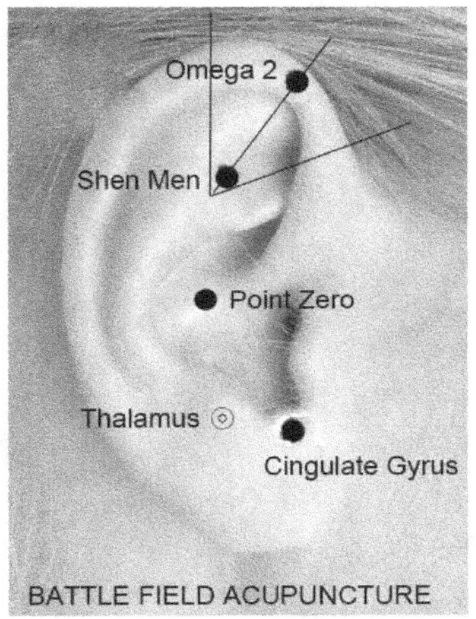

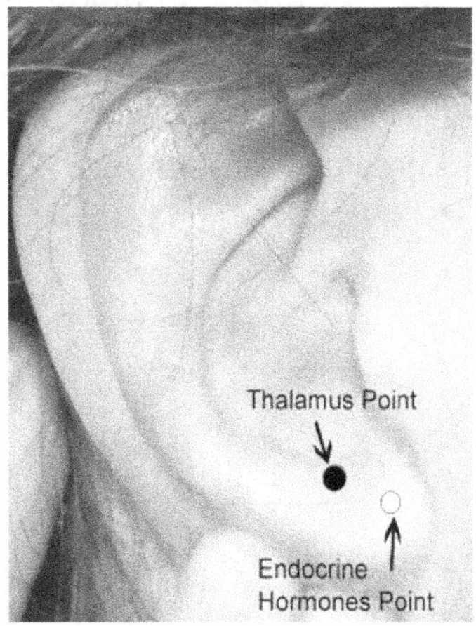

[Point Location]

Cingulate Gyrus:
Bisect intertragal-notch
 Find cartilage ring
 Lower edge of cartilage
Needle base, outside edge of cartilage

Omega 2:
Locate apex of ear and connection point to face.
Halfway in between
Needle crown of pinna

Point Zero:
Follow root of helix, in the root past the groove
Needle 2-4mm posterior past groove .

Shen Men (Spirit Gate) :

Acupoint Magnet Therapy

This point is located in the triangular fossa, superior to the origin of the superior and inferior crus of the antihelix.

Thalamus Point (Pain Control Point, Sub-cortex, Brain Point):
This point is located at the bottom of the inside wall of anti-tragus where the anti-tragus meets the concha, directly below the apex of the antitragus. Sometimes you may feel an indentation.

[INDICATION]

Cingulate Gyrus:
General sedation effect
Relaxation
Anxiety/Stress Reduction
Reduces high blood pressure

Thalamus:
Represents the whole diencephalon, including the thalamus and the hypothalamus.
Pre-amplifies signals sent to the cerebral cortex.
Eliminates meaningless background noise.
Highest level of the supraspinal gate control system
Acute and chronic pain

Omega 2:
Reduces inflammatory reactions.

Point Zero:
Geometrical and physiological center of the whole auricle
Creates balance and homeostasis.
Balances energy, hormones and brain activity.
Supports the other auricular points.

Shen Men:
Tranquilizes the mind and allows a harmonious connection to the spirit.
Alleviates stress, pain, tension, anxiety, depression, insomnia, restlessness, and excessive sensitivity.
Universal point useful for auricular analgesia

Acupoint Magnet Therapy

Pain, tension, anxiety, and depression.
Drug, alcohol detoxification

These 5 points protocol was developed by USAF COL (ret) Richard
Niemtzok, MD and has been used extensively for PTSD in the military as
well as in the VA Healthcare System.

 Among these points Thalamus and Cingulate Gyrus are the most
effective points to relieve chronic pain. Stimulation of these points
results in Central Desensitization of this brain area to relieve chronic
pain.

Thalamus

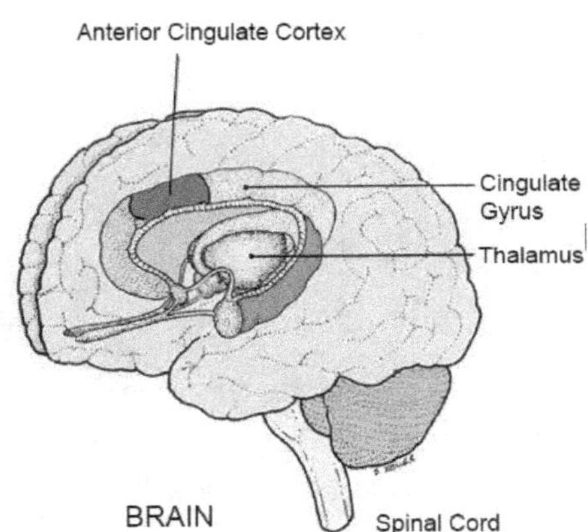

The thalamus is a small structure within the brain located just above the brain stem between the cerebral cortex and the midbrain and has extensive nerve connections to both. The main function of the thalamus is to relay motor and sensory signals to the cerebral cortex. It also regulates sleep, alertness and wakefulness.

Pain sensation from the body is relayed primarily at the VPL (ventral
posterior lateral) nuclei of the thalamus. Deep brain stimulation of the
VPL has been shown to improve measures of pain in patients with
neuropathic pain.
Chronic pain from a variety of causes can be alleviated by stimulating
the thalamus point in the auricle.

The cingulate cortex

The cingulate cortex is a part of the brain situated in the medial aspect
of the cerebral cortex. The cingulate cortex includes the entire **cingulate
gyrus**, which lies immediately above the corpus callosum, and the

continuation of this in the cingulate sulcus. The cingulate cortex is usually considered part of the limbic lobe.

Cingulate Gyrus and the Limbic System: Gyrus is a fold or "bulge" in the brain. The cingulate gyrus is the curved fold covering the corpus callosum. A component of the limbic system, it is involved in processing **emotions and behavior regulation**. It also helps to regulate autonomic motor function.
Damage to the cingulate gyrus may result in cognitive, emotional, and behavioral disorders.

Functions:
Coordinates Sensory Input with Emotions
Emotional Responses to Pain
Regulates Aggressive Behavior.
Communication
Maternal Bonding
Language expression
Decision Making

Cingulate Gyrus Dysfunction
Emotional and behavioral disorders relating to the cingulate gyrus include depression, anxiety disorders, and obsessive-compulsive disorders. Cingulate gyrus dysfunction has also been linked to attention deficit disorders, schizophrenia, psychiatric disorders, and autism.

Individuals with an improperly functioning Cingulate Gyrus often have problems communicating and dealing with changing situations. Under such conditions, they may become angry or easily frustrated and have emotional or violent outbursts.

Physiologically, individuals may experience **chronic pain** or display addictive behaviors such as drug or alcohol abuse and eating disorders.

CHAPTER THREE

3-1. Meridians

The Twelve Principal Meridians

There are twelve principal meridians throughout the body. Each of the twelve Principal Meridian is named after the six Yin organs (Liver, Heart, Kidney, Spleen, Lung and Pericardium), and the six Yang organs (Large Intestine, Small Intestine, Stomach, Urinary Bladder, Gall bladder and Triple Burner (San Jiao)) The Triple Burner (San Jiao) is an imaginary organ system that has no anatomical counterpart in the Western medicine, but also related to the physiology in the body in the TCM.

The energetic integrity of the each meridian reflects the condition of the organ system and the muscular system along the pathway of the meridian. Stimulation of Acupuncture points on the meridians offer the means of balancing the Qi in the meridians and organ systems

The following explains the functionality of each meridian and the symptoms accompanied by when the meridian Qi is excess or deficient due to any pathological causes. A simple treatment protocol is based on the idea when Qi is excess, drain it (sedation), and when Qi is deficient, supplement it (tonification). An acupuncturist can find problem meridians by analyzing the signs and symptoms observed from the patient and treat disorders by inserts needles at the appropriate acupuncture points to correct them..

3-1-1. THE LUNG MERIDIAN (Fei JIng 肺經, 手太陰肺經)

Functions: :
The lungs Qi controls breath and energy, and assists the heart

with the circulation of blood. The Internal Medicine Classic states: "Qi is the commander of blood; when Qi moves, Blood follows. Blood is the mother of Qi; where Blood goes, Qi follows."

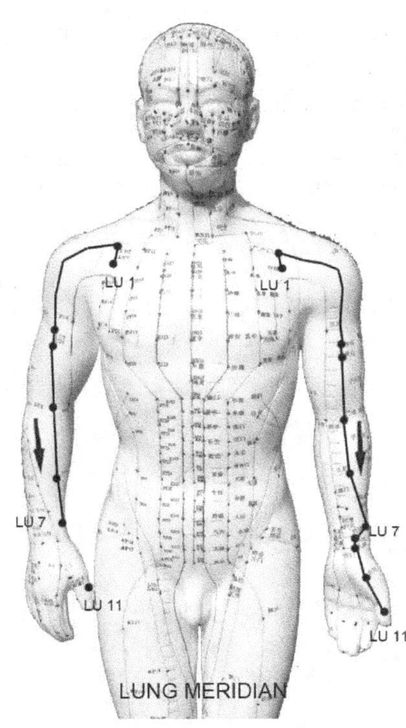

The lungs also control the skin pores and is responsible for adjusting body temperature through perspiration and shivering. The skin is the first line of defense against noxious environmental energies such as heat and cold. Flu and the common cold are caused by impairment of Wei Qi (skin's protective energy) to resist the external invasion. Symptoms of these diseases usually settle in the lungs.

Pale skin and poor complexion are common indications of weak lungs Qi. The nose is the external aperture of the lungs and the gate of breath. A clogged or runny nose is another indicator of weak lungs.

A person, grief-stricken and steeped in sadness, may cause Lung Qi stagnation. They may have trouble letting go.

When the Lung Qi is weak, there can be illnesses of the lungs; asthma, allergies, and frequent colds.

The Lung meridian rules the skin; so rashes, eczema, and problems with too much sweating or too little sweating may occur.

Excess and Deficiency Symptoms of the Lung meridian

MERIDIAN	STATUS	INDICATIONS
Lung	Deficiency	lethargy, night sweat, anxious, restlessness, loose stool, insomnia, dry throat, numbness of the limbs, Headache, breathing difficulty,, asthma, bronchitis.
	Excess	shortness of breath, cough, chest pain or congestion,, itchy skin, skin disorder, cold, constipation, indigestion, little sweat, nasal congestion, asthma, bronchitis,

3-1-2. THE LARGE INTESTINE MERIDIAN (手陽明大腸經)

Functions:

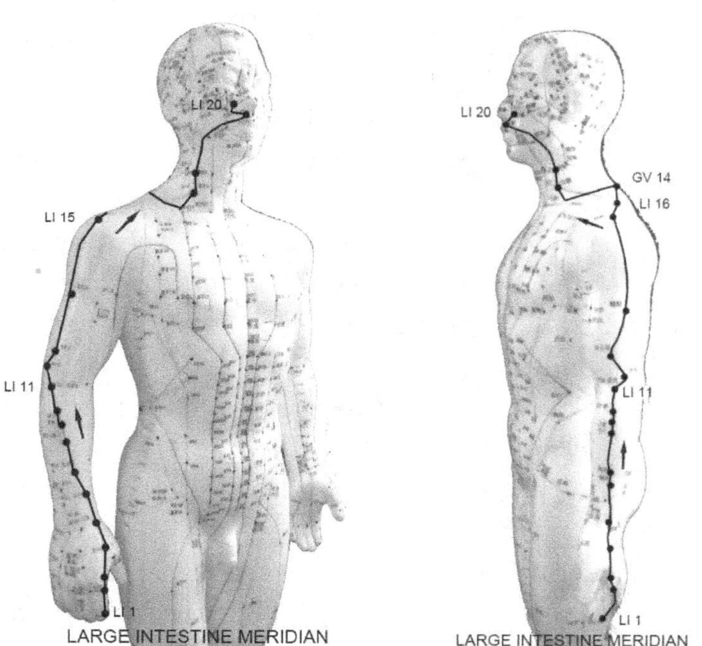

The large intestine controls the transformation of digestive wastes from liquid to solid state and transports the solids out for excretion. It plays a major role in the balance of bodily fluids and assists the lungs in controlling the skin's pores and perspiration.

Coupled with the lungs, the large intestine depends on the lungs for movement via the expansion and contraction of the diaphragm, which works like a pump to give impetus to peristalsis by regulating abdominal pressure. Thus sluggish bowels may be stimulated and constipation can be relieved by deep diaphragmatic breathing and by tonifying the lung meridian. Conversely, congested lungs may be cleared by purging the bowels.

Excess and Deficiency Symptoms of the Large Intestine Meridian

MERIDIAN	STATUS	INDICATIONS
Large Intestine	Deficiency	constipation, low abdominal pain, diarrhea, frequent urination, stroke, Bell's palsy
	Excess	low abdominal distension, dizziness, headache, migraine, itchy skin, skin disorder, arthritis, obesity.

3-1-3. THE STOMACH MERIDIAN (足陽明胃經)

Functions:

The stomach is called the "Minister of the Mill" and is also known as the "Sea of Nourishment". It is responsible for providing the entire system with energy from the digestion of food and fluids.

Those with weak Stomach Qi may crave sweets. Excessive mucus may collect in the lungs or in the sinuses.

Common symptoms include; Fatigue, diarrhea, gas and bloating, food allergies or food sensitivities, eating disorders, heartburn, and canker sores.

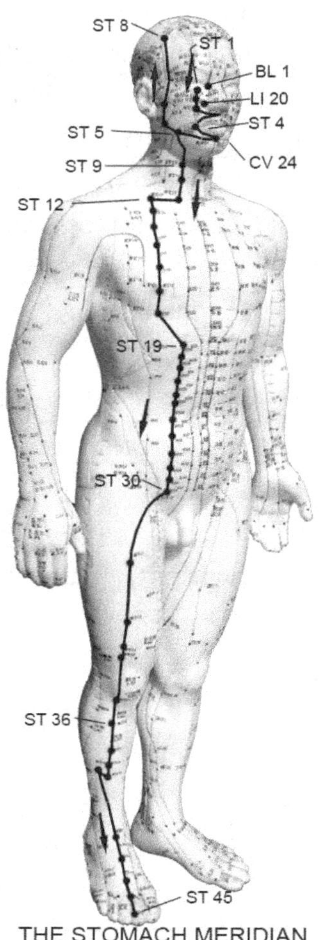

THE STOMACH MERIDIAN

Excess and Deficiency Symptoms of the Stomach Meridian

MERIDIAN	STATUS	INDICATIONS
Stomach	Deficiency	cold body, cold low abdomen, weak muscle and limbs, low energy.
	Excess	big appetite, gastritis and duodenitis, heartburn, diarrhea, constipation, indigestion, abdominal pain.

3-1-4. THE SPLEEN MERIDIAN (足太陰脾經)

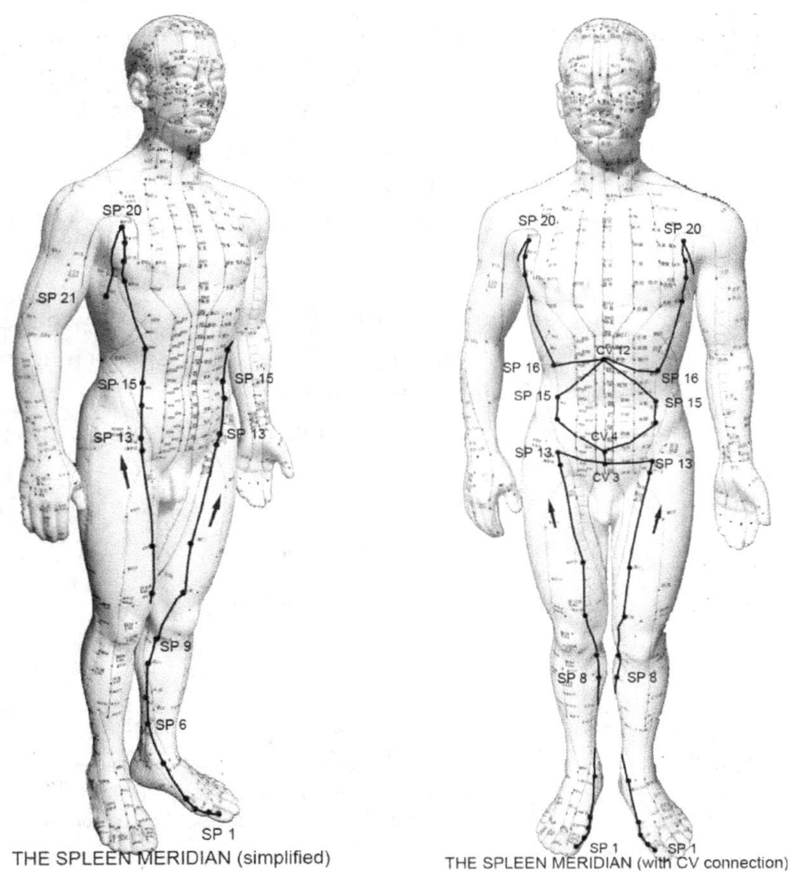

THE SPLEEN MERIDIAN (simplified)   THE SPLEEN MERIDIAN (with CV connection)

Functions:

The spleen is the largest organ in the lymphatic system. It is an important organ for keeping bodily fluids balanced, but it is possible to live without it. People can live without the spleen because other organs, such as the liver and lymph nodes, can take over the duties of the spleen. But people will be more at risk to develop infections without the spleen.

The spleen plays multiple supporting roles in the body. It acts as a filter for blood as part of the immune system. Old red blood cells are recycled in the spleen, and platelets and white blood cells are stored there.

In TCM (Traditional Chinese medicine), since the Spleen meridian includes the pancreas, its physiological function is associated with digestion as well as blood management. The Spleen meridian regulates the quantity and quality of blood in circulation and coordinates with the kidneys to control fluid balance throughout the system. Edema is attributed to the Spleen and the weak Kidney function.
The spleen energy is reflected by the tone and condition of muscle tissue. Weak limbs and muscular atrophy are indications of deficient spleen energy.

Spleen and pancreas condition are reflected externally by the color and tone of the lips: reddish moist lips indicate strong spleen function; pale dry lips are a sign of weak spleen function.
The mouth is the spleen's external aperture, people with strong Spleen energy may become a good singer.
Temperamental moodiness is the Spleen associated emotion. The Chinese term for 'bad temper' is 'bad spleen energy'(脾气不好的 pí qi bù hǎo de), a similar English term 'splenetic'.

Excess and deficiency Symptoms of the Spleen meridian

MERIDIAN	STATUS	INDICATIONS
Spleen	Deficiency	pensiveness, indigestion, abdominal pain, bloating, dry mouth, cold lower limbs, forgetfulness, loss of appetite, insomnia, emaciation.
	Excess	Pensive and restless, weight gain, feeling of heaviness of the body, bloating, joint pain (knee / ankle), arthritis, over sleeping, feeling of heaviness of the legs.

3-1-5. THE HEART MERIDIAN (手少陰心經)

Functions:
The heart controls the circulation and distribution of blood, and therefore, all the other organs depend upon it. The heart is not just a

pumping machine, its function is also associated with the wellbeing of mind and emotions.

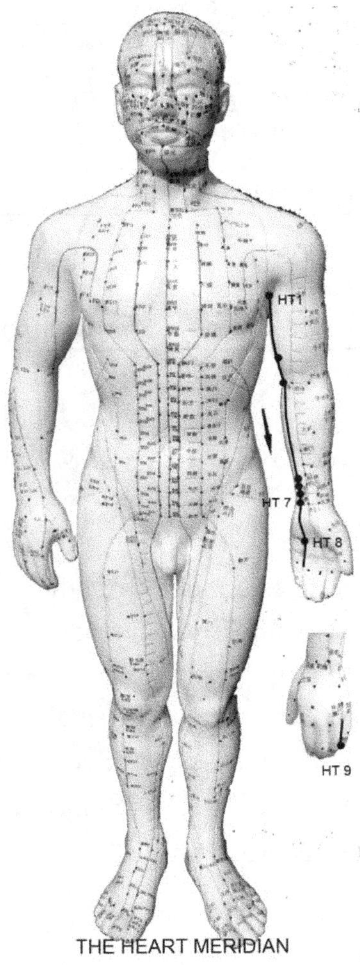

The Internal Medicine Classic(黃帝內經 Huang Di Nei Jing, Yellow Emperor's Internal Canon, medical text, 300 BC) states: "The Heart commands all of the organs and viscera, houses the spirit, and controls the emotions.'"

In Chinese, the word for Heart (心 Xin) is also used to denote Mind. When the heart is strong and steady, it controls the emotions; when it is weak and wavering, the emotions rebel and prey upon the heart, then the heart loses its command over the body. Emotional stress literally can break the heart.

The condition of the heart is reflected on the tongue. The color and texture of the tongue indicates the condition of the heart. The facial complexion, which is a direct reflection of blood circulation, is also an external indicator of heart function. When the Heart Qi is weak, a person may be lack luster, or appear bland in color. They may suffer from anxiety or restlessness. They may be too excitable, or they may be emotionally cold and unfeeling.

Excess and Deficiency Symptoms of the Heart meridian

MERIDIAN	STATUS	INDICATIONS
Heart	Deficiency	restlessness, easily frightened, cold hands and feet, poor circulation, insomnia, lethargy, sweaty palm, chest pain, palpitation, forgetfulness, hypotension, migraine.
	Excess	stroke, angina pectoris, arrhythmia, restlessness , anxiety, hot palm, dizziness, shortness of breath, headache, hypertension

3-1-6. THE SMALL INTESTINE MERIDIAN (手太陽小腸經)

Functions:

The small intestine receives partially digested food from the stomach and further refines it, then assimilates the purified nutrients and moves the wastes to the large intestine for elimination. Paired with the Heart by Fire energy, the small intestine is associated with the emotion sadness, as reflected in the Chinese term "the pain of Duan Chang" (斷肠 broken intestines), which is equivalent to the English term "broken heart".

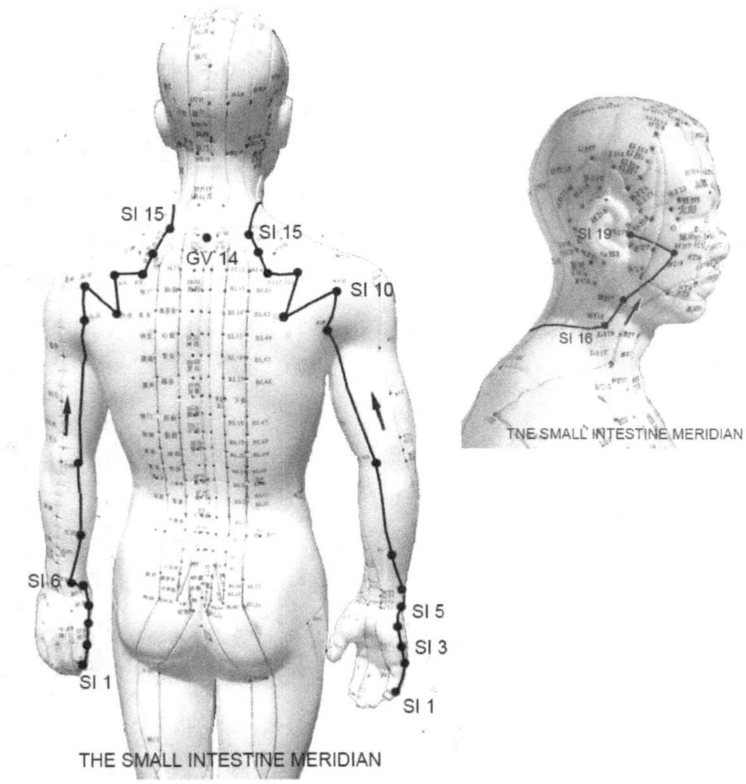

Excess and Deficiency Symptoms of the Small Intestine Meridian

MERIDIAN	STATUS	INDICATIONS
Small Intestine	Deficiency	pale complexion, emaciation, anemia, loss of energy, lethargy, dizziness, hair loss.
	Excess	dysmenorrhea, irregular menstrual cycle, dysuria, headache, indigestion, low abdominal pain, stiffness of neck, , shoulder(scapula) pain, knee pain, migraine, back pain

3-1-7. THE URINARY BLADDER MERIDIAN (足太陽膀胱經)

Functions

The urinary bladder as an organ has the function of storing and excreting urinary waste fluids from the kidneys, but as an energy system the urinary bladder meridian is intimately related to the functions of the autonomic nervous system. That's because the urinary bladder meridian runs along the back of the body from head to the low back alongside of the spinal column, and to the heel and foot. The acupuncture points of the urinary bladder meridian exert a direct influence on the sympathetic and parasympathetic trunks of the autonomic nervous system

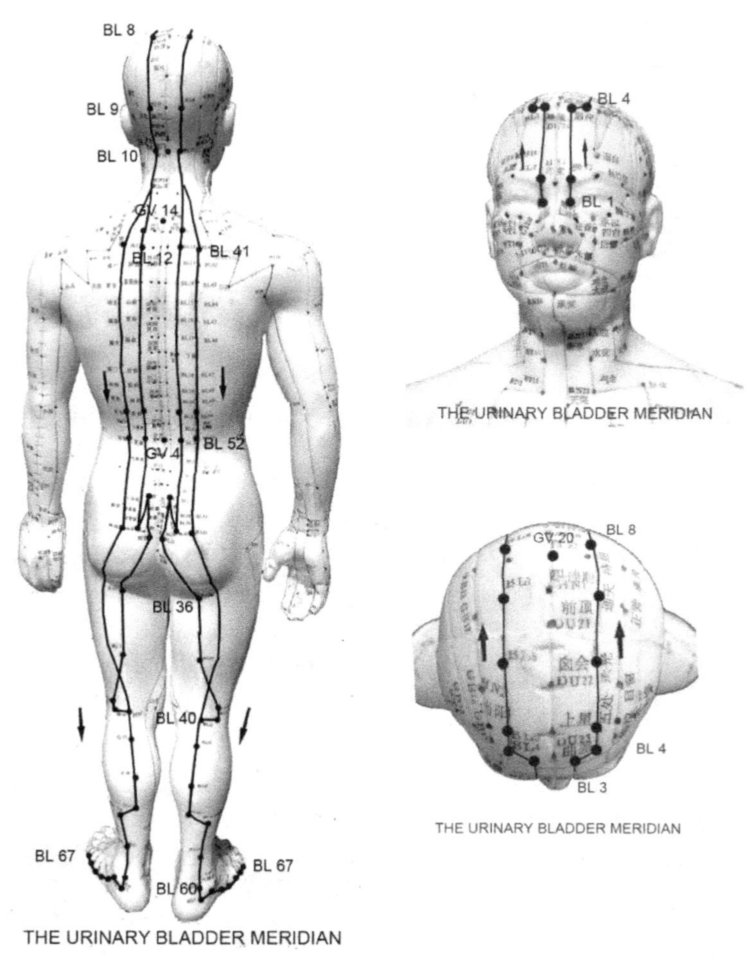

Excess and Deficiency Symptoms of the Urinary Bladder Meridian.

MERIDIAN	STATUS	INDICATIONS
Urinary Bladder	Deficiency	nervousness, neurosis, easily frightened, headache, stuffy nose, low abdominal pain, edema, frequent urination, waist pain, dysuria, back pain, walking difficulty, blurry vision, hemorrhoid, cystitis.
	Excess	nervousness, over-sensitive, headache(back of head), back pain, sciatica, stiffness of nape, acute cystitis, stuffy nose, nose bleeding,

3-1-8. THE KIDNEY MERIDIAN (足少陰腎經)

Functions:

Kidney is regarded as the reservoir of essential energy. The original prenatal energy (Yuan Qi) which forms the basis of life, is stored in the kidneys, which is why the kidneys are also known as the Root of Life.

The kidney meridian system also includes the adrenal glands. These glands sit like hats on top of the kidneys and secrete a wide range of essential hormones that regulate metabolism, excretion, immunity, sexual potency and fertility. The kidney meridian system also includes the testicles in men, and the ovaries in women. Thus the kidneys control sexual and reproductive functions, and provide the body's prime source of sexual vitality. The kidneys are responsible for filtering waste metabolites from the blood and moving them to the bladder for excretion in urine. The kidneys control the balance of fluids in the body. they regulate the body's acid-alkaline balance (pH) by selectively filtering out or retaining various minerals.

The kidneys, and particularly the adrenal glands, are especially vulnerable to damage from excessive stress and sexual activity. Such damage is a major cause of immune deficiency, low vitality, and sexual impotence.

The kidneys control the growth and development of bones, and nourish the marrow, which is the body's source of red and white blood cells. Weak kidney energy is therefore a prime cause of anemia and immune deficiency.

The spinal cord and the brain are forms of marrow, and therefore, poor memory, inability to think clearly, and backache are all regarded as indicators of impaired kidney function and deficient kidney energy.

The Kidneys provide the capacity and drive for strength, skill and hard work. A patient with strong Kidneys can work hard and purposefully for long periods of time. A patient with weak Kidneys will lack strength and endurance.

Kidney vitality is reflected externally by the condition of head and body hair and is associated with the ears. Kidney Qi declines with aging, so there may be hearing loss or ringing in the ears with aging. For female when the Kidney yin declines, they may experience menopause, hot flashes, night sweats, dry skin and mucous membranes.

Kidney Yang weakness is associated with cold extremities, cold belly, declining sexual vigor, and urinary frequency or incontinence.

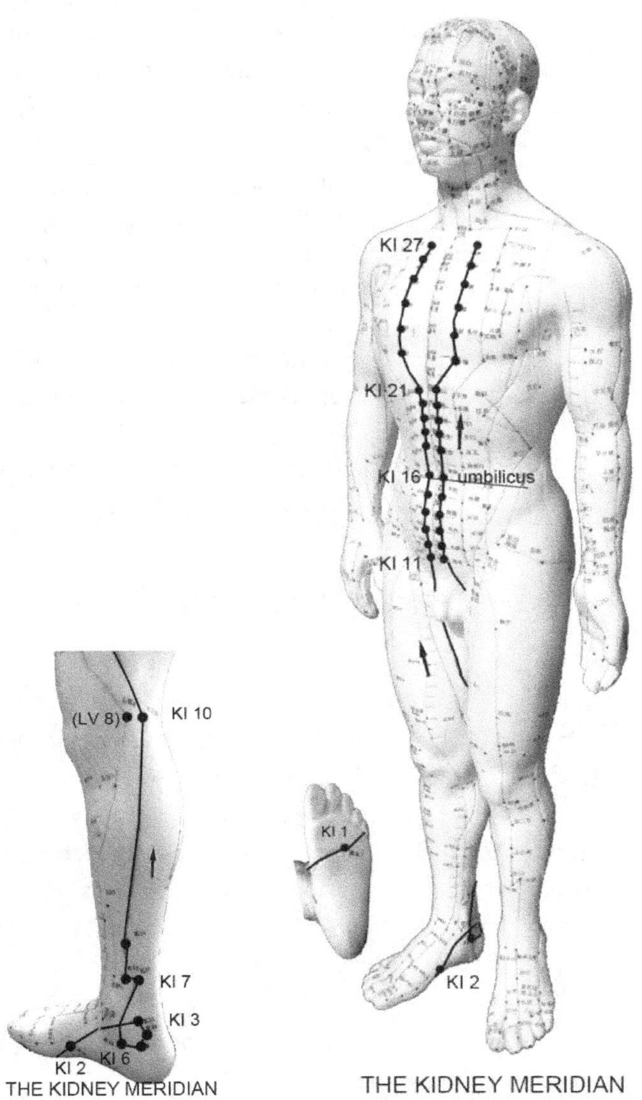

THE KIDNEY MERIDIAN

THE KIDNEY MERIDIAN

Excess and Deficiency Symptoms of the Kidney Meridian

MERIDIAN	STATUS	INDICATIONS
Kidney	Deficiency	anxious, impatient, no motivation, dull complexion, lack of energy, low back pain, tinnitus, hearing loss impotence,, forgetfulness, cough, cold limbs.
	Excess	restlessness, nervousness, angry, swelling of limbs, dizziness, grey complexion, tinnitus, easily get tired, nephritis, edema, irregular menses, allergic rhinitis, dysuria, frequent urination, hypertension, hypotension, allergy, dysmenorrhea, lack of energy, shortness of breath, abdominal distension, sole (feverish, pain, tingling).

3-1-9. THE LIVER MERIDIAN (足厥陰肝經)

Functions:
The liver is responsible for filtering, detoxifying, nourishing, replenishing, and storing blood. The liver stores large amounts of sugar in the form of glycogen, which it releases into the blood stream as glucose whenever the body requires extra infusions of metabolic energy. The liver controls the peripheral nervous system, which regulates muscular activity and tension. The inability to relax is often caused by liver dysfunction. Liver energy also controls ligaments and tendons, which together with muscles regulate motor activity and determine physical coordination.
Liver function is reflected externally in the condition of finger and toenails, and by the eyes and vision.

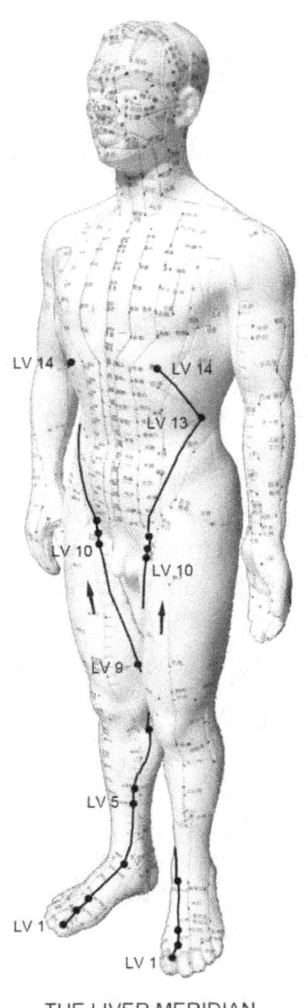

THE LIVER MERIDIAN

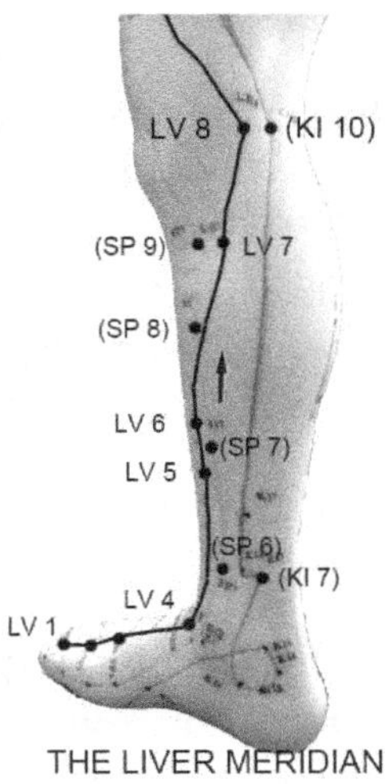

THE LIVER MERIDIAN

Excess and Deficiency Symptoms of the Liver meridian

MERIDIAN	STATUS	INDICATIONS
Liver	Deficiency	fatigue, loss of appetite, neurosis, headache, restlessness, irritable, dizziness, insomnia, night blindness, muscle spasm, migraine.
	Excess	easily get excited or angry, hepatitis, cirrhosis, headache, insomnia, eye disorder, trigeminal neuralgia, spasm / tingling of the limbs, muscle pain, indigestion, heartburn, fatigue, vomiting, belching, gastritis, abdominal pain, chronic diarrhea,

3-1-10. THE GALLBLADDER MERIDIAN (足少陽膽經)

Functions:

The gallbladder serves as a reservoir for bile while it is not being used for digestion. The gallbladder's absorbent lining concentrates the stored bile. When food enters the small intestine, a hormone called cholecystokinin is released, signaling the gallbladder to contract and secrete bile into the small intestine through the common bile duct.

The bile helps the digestive process by breaking up fats. It also drains waste products from the liver into the duodenum, a part of the small intestine.

In TCM, the common tension headache is caused by obstruction in the gall-bladder meridian, which runs up over the shoulders and back of the neck to the top of the head and forehead. Hence such headaches are usually accompanied by neck and shoulder tension.

Excess and Deficiency Symptoms of the Gallbladder meridian

MERIDIAN	STATUS	INDICATIONS
Gall Bladder	Deficiency	easily frightened, timid, incisiveness, low motivation, insomnia, indigestion, migraine, constipation or diarrhea, migraine,
	Excess	anxious, easily get angry, headache, hearing loss, tinnitus, eye pain, back pain, sciatica,, hypochondriac region pain.

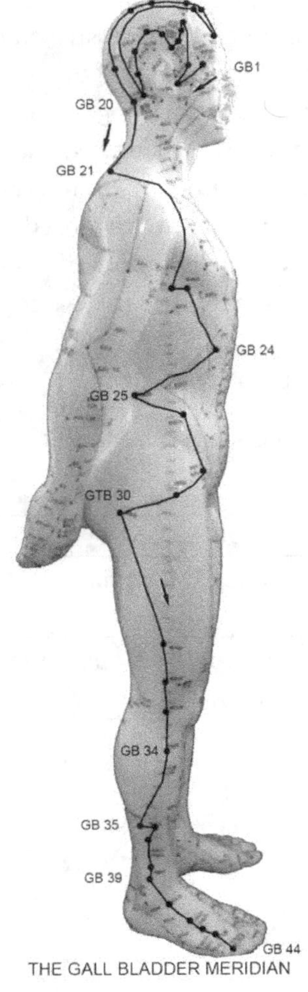

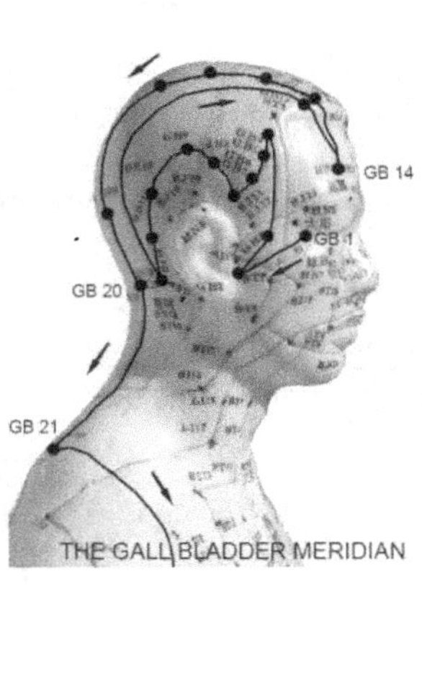

3-1-11. **THE PERICARDIUM MERIDIAN** (手厥陰心包經)

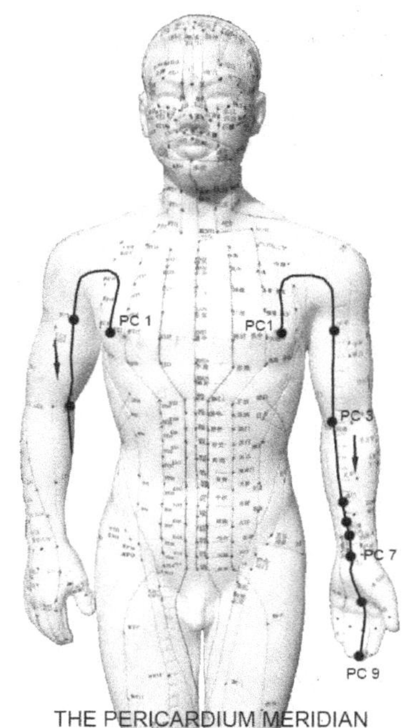

Functions:

The pericardium is the heart's protective sack. Although it is not recognized as an organ in Western physiology, it is regarded in Chinese medicine as Fire-energy organ whose special function is to protect the heart. Not only does the pericardium provide the heart with physical protection, its energy also protects the heart from damage and disruption by excessive emotional energies generated by the other organs, such as anger from the liver, fear from the kidneys, and grief from the lungs. Extreme outbursts of emotions are regarded as powerful disruptors of internal energy balance and major causes of disease. Without the pericardium to protect it, the heart would be subjected to injury from the radical fluctuations of energy caused by every emotional change.

Excess and Deficiency Symptoms of the Pericardium Meridian

MERIDIAN	STATUS	INDICATIONS
Pericardium	Deficiency	hot palm, neurosis, insomnia, hypotension.
	Excess	arrhythmia, angina pectoris, palpitation, hypertension, dizziness,

3-1-12. THE TRIPLE BURNER (OR WARMER) MERIDIAN (手少陽三焦經)

Functions:

In Chinese 'San' means three, 'Jiao' means 'burn'. San Jiao is

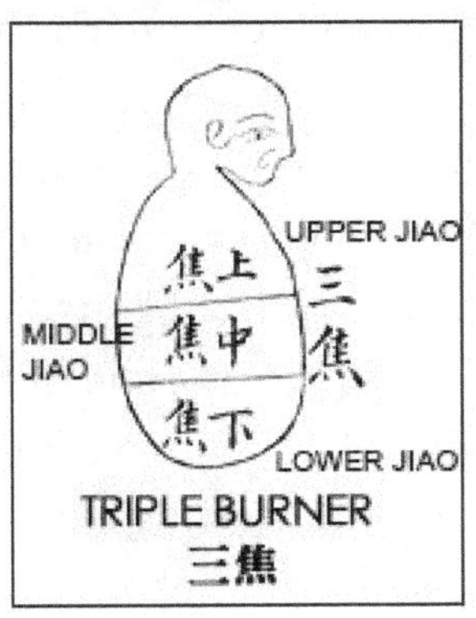

originally referred to as the 'Triple Burner', but 'Triple Warmer' or 'Triple Heater' is also used.

The Triple Burner (San Jiao) is a special concept in TCM, and there is no corresponding organ in the western anatomy.

The triple burner is actually a collective term tor the upper, middle and lower burner. The upper burner is located above the diaphragm and includes the heart and lungs. The middle burner is located in the region above the belly button and below the diaphragm and includes the spleen and stomach. The Lower burner is located below the belly button, and it includes the liver, kidneys, large intestine, small intestine and bladder. The function of sexual organs and reproductive organs is also controlled by the lower burner. The Triple Burner represents collective harmonizing function of organs in the three different parts of the body.

The Triple Burner is a collective system through which water, food and fluid are transported, as well as responsible for the production and circulation of nourishing energy. The upper burner acts like a mist. The middle burner acts like foam. The Lower burner acts like a swamp. The Triple Burner also controls the entire circulation of body fluid.

Therefore, disharmony of the Triple Burner can lead to edema or difficult urination.

The Triple Burner is also responsible for the production and circulation of nourishing energy (營氣 Ying Qi) and protective energy (衛氣 Wei Qi).

On a psychological level, the Triple Burner can move Qi and lift depression derived from stagnation of Liver Qi. When the Triple Burners are full, the consciousness becomes stable and the Mind's intent is benevolent and kindhearted. The Triple Burners are also linked with the Heart and Pericardium and are affected by the emotion of joy. When the energy of the heart is strong and pure (without guilt), and the desires and thoughts of an individual are at peace, then the energy of the sexual essence (Jing) will spread into the Triple Burners, and the Blood will flourish within the meridians.

If the "fire of desire" is combined with the energy of the Triple Burners, the energy of sexual essence will overflow, mixing itself with the energy of Ming Men and will leave the body via the reproductive organs

Excess and Deficiency Symptoms of the Triple Burner Meridian

MERIDIAN	STATUS	INDICATIONS
Triple Burner	Deficiency	headache, dizziness, tinnitus, allergy, .menstrual disorder, fatigue.
	Excess	migraine, stiff neck, trigeminal neuralgia, low abdominal pain, shoulder pain, dysmenorrhea, amenorrhea, infertility, digestive system disorders.

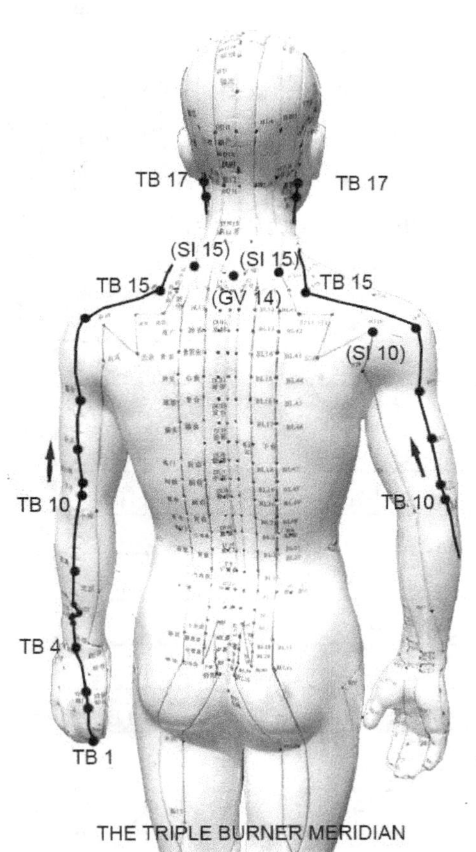

TB 17
TB 17
(SI 15)
(SI 15)
TB 15
TB 15
(GV 14)
(SI 10)
TB 10
TB 10
TB 4
TB 1
THE TRIPLE BURNER MERIDIAN

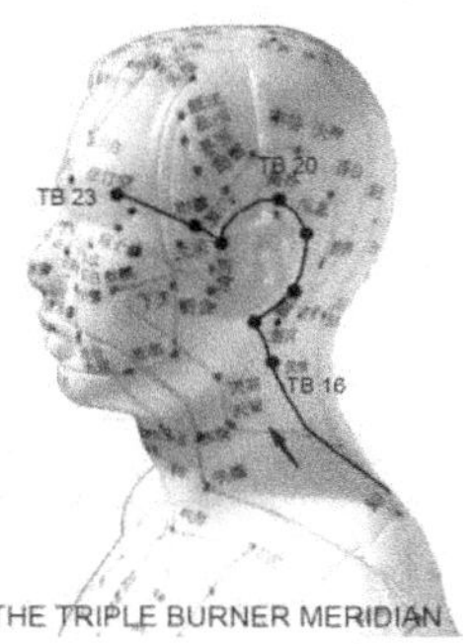

TB 20
TB 23
TB 16
THE TRIPLE BURNER MERIDIAN

3-2. Treatment Protocol:
Tonification / Sedation of the 12 Principal Meridians

Once excess and deficient condition of a meridian is found, acupuncturist can treat this with selection of appropriate acupuncture points. Here is an example of the Five Phase Acupuncture (Sa Ahm Acupuncture) technique. The complete detail of the Five Phase Acupuncture (Sa Ahm Acupuncture) is introduced in the book "Meridian Therapy Handbook – Tune-up Your Body".

TONIFICATION	STEP 1	STEP 2	STEP 3	STEP 4
MERIDIAN	Tonify	Sedate	Tonify	Sedate
LUNG	LU 9	LU 10	SP 3	HT 8
LARGE INT.	LI 11	LI 5	ST 36	SI 5
STOMACH	ST 41	ST 43	SI 5	GB 41
SPLEEN	SP 2	SP 1	HT 8	LV 1
HEART	HT 9	HT 3	LV 1	KI 10
SMALL INT.	SI 3	SI 2	GB 41	BL66
URINARY BLADDER	BL67	BL40	LI 1	ST 36
KIDNEY	KI 7	KI 3	LU 8	SP 3
PERICARDIUM	PC 9	PC 3	LV 1	KI 10
SAN JIAO	TB 3	TB 2	GB 41	BL66
GALL BLADDER	GB 43	GB 44	BL66	LI 1
LIVER	LV 8	LV 4	KI 10	LU 8

SEDATION	STEP 1	STEP 2	STEP 3	STEP 4
MERIDIAN	Sedate	Tonify	Sedate	Tonify
LUNG	LU 5	LU 10	KI 10	HT 8
LARGE INT.	LI 2	LI 5	BL66	SI 5
STOMACH	ST 45	ST 43	LI 1	GB 41
SPLEEN	SP 5	SP 1	LU 8	LV 1
HEART	HT 7	HT 3	SP 3	KI 10
SMALL INT.	SI 8	SI 2	ST 36	BL66
URINARY BLADDER	BL65	BL40	GB 41	ST 36
KIDNEY	KI 1	Kd 3	LV 1	SP 3
PERICARDIUM	PC 7	PC 3	SP 3	KI 10
SAN JIAO	TB 10	TB 2	ST 36	BL66
GALL BLADDER	GB 38	GB 44	SI 5	LI 1
LIVER	LV 2	LV 4	HT 8	LU 8

3-3. YUAN (原) SOURCE POINTS AND INDICATIONS

Yuan (原) Source Points are where the Yuan Qi, the body's primordial Qi, pools. Each of the 12 regular meridians has a Yuan (Source) point located near the wrist or ankle joints through which the vital energy of the Zang Fu organs passes and to some extent accumulates.

Pathological changes of the Zang Fu organs are often manifested at the Yuan (source) points. For example, tenderness at a Yuan (source) point often indicates pathological changes of the related Zang Fu organs.

 The 12 Yuan (source) points are included in the category of the

Five Shu Points. **Each Yang meridian has its own Yuan (source) point, which is located between the Shu-stream point and the Jing-River point.** The 6 Yin meridians do not have separate Yuan (source) points, their Shu-stream points are Yuan (source) points. The Yuan (source) points and Shu-stream points of Yin meridians are the same.

Yin Yuan Source Points can be used to tonify the 5 Yin Organs (HT, LU, SP, KD, and LV). The Yang Yuan Source Points are not used to tonify yang organs, but can be used to expel pathogenic factors or release excess patterns.

Yin Yuan Source Points: LU 9, PC 7, HT 7, LV 3, SP 3, KI 3
Yang Yuan Source Points: LI 4, TB 4, SI 4, ST 42, GB 40, BL64

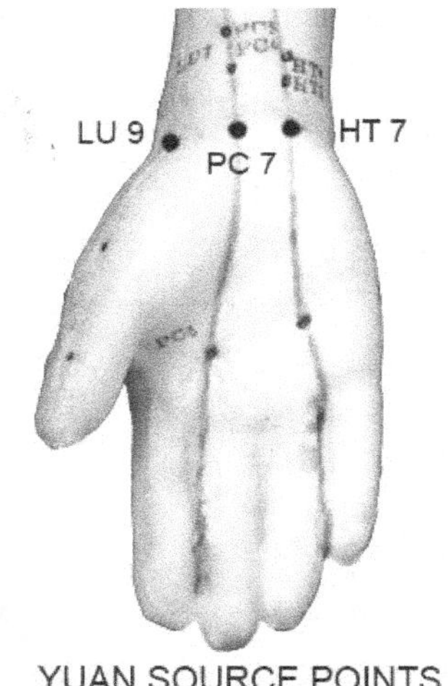

YUAN SOURCE POINTS

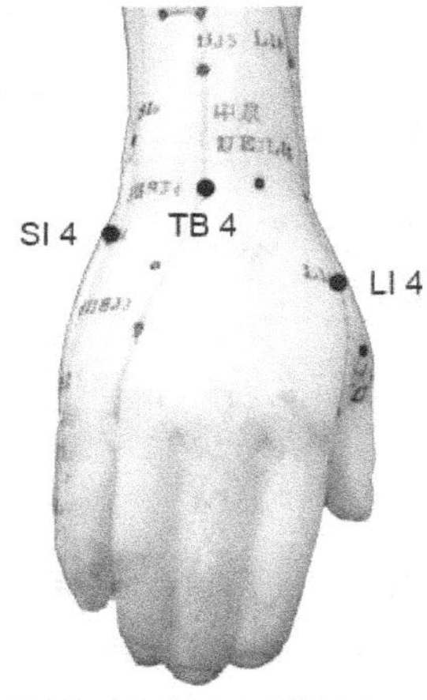

YUAN SOURCE POINTS

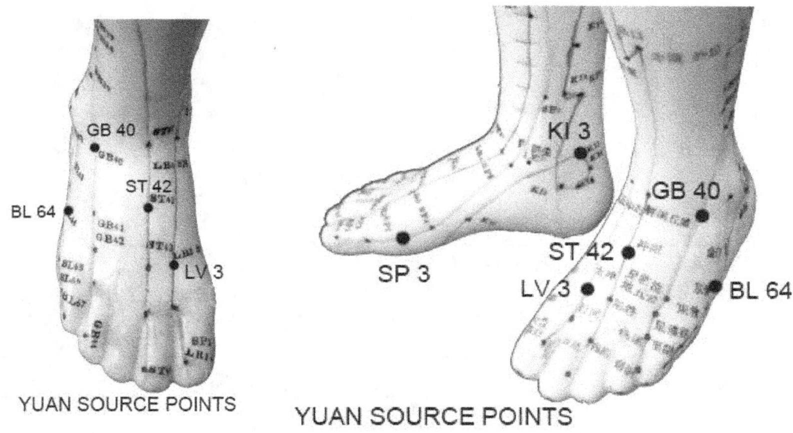
GB 40
ST 42
BL 64
LV 3
YUAN SOURCE POINTS
KI 3
GB 40
ST 42
SP 3
LV 3
BL 64
YUAN SOURCE POINTS

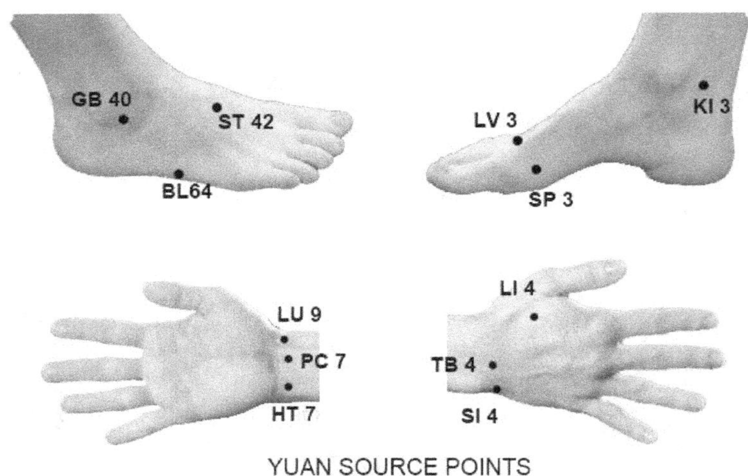

YUAN SOURCE POINT: Yang Meridians			
acne	LI 4	He Gu	合谷
allergies	LI 4	He Gu	合谷
arm problems	SI 4	Wangu	腕骨
bell's palsy	ST 42	Chongyang	沖陽
chest pain.	BL 64	Jinggu	京骨
Chronic Pain	LI 4	He Gu	合谷
eye problems	LI 4	He Gu	合谷
foot pain	ST 42	Chongyang	沖陽
hand and wrist problems	SI 4	Wangu	腕骨
hay fever	LI 4	He Gu	合谷
headache	SI 4	Wangu	腕骨
headache,	LI 4	He Gu	合谷
irritability	BL 64	Jinggu	京骨
lower limbs a/or ankle problem	GB 40	Qiuxu	丘墟
mental confusion	BL 64	Jinggu	京骨
neck pain	SI 4	Wangu	腕骨
palpitations	BL 64	Jinggu	京骨
regulates water metabolism	TB 4	Yangchi	陽池
rhinitis	LI 4	He Gu	合谷

shoulder problem	SI 4	Wangu	腕骨
wrist problem	TB 4	Yangchi	陽池

SHU STREAM (Yuan SOURCE POINTS: Yin Meridians by INDICATION			
abdominal, or epigastric pain	SP 3	Taibai	太白
amenorrhea	LV 3	Taichong	太沖
anger	LV 3	Taichong	太沖
angina	HT 7	Sherman	神門
ankle pain	KI 3	Taixi	太谿
anxiety	HT 7	Sherman	神門
anxiety	KI 3	Taixi	太谿
anxiety.	LV 3	Taichong	太沖
asthma	LU 9	Taiyuan	太淵
Asthma	KI 3	Taixi	太谿
breast tenderness.	LV 3	Taichong	太沖
Carpal Tunnel Syndrome	PC 7	Daling	大陵
cough	LU 9	Taiyuan	太淵
digestive issues	SP 3	Taibai	太白
dizziness	LV 3	Taichong	太沖
dizziness,	KI 3	Taixi	太谿
dysmenorrhea.	LV 3	Taichong	太沖
excessive dream	KI 3	Taixi	太谿
frequent urination	KI 3	Taixi	太谿
frequent urination	KI 3	Taixi	太谿
headache	KI 3	Taixi	太谿
headaches	LV 3	Taichong	太沖
heart pain.	SP 3	Taibai	太白
heaviness in the body	SP 3	Taibai	太白
insomnia	HT 7	Sherman	神門
insomnia	KI 3	Taixi	太谿
insomnia	PC 7	Daling	大陵
insomnia	LV 3	Taichong	太沖
irregular heart beat	HT 7	Sherman	神門
irritability	LV 3	Taichong	太沖

Acupoint Magnet Therapy

Low back pain	KI 3	Taixi	太谿
mania	HT 7	Sherman	神門
Manic psychosis	PC 7	Daling	大陵
pain in the chest and hypochondrium	PC 7	Daling	大陵
painful eyes	LV 3	Taichong	太沖
palpitations	HT 7	Sherman	神門
palpitations	PC 7	Daling	大陵
PMS	LV 3	Taichong	太沖
shortness of breathing	LU 9	Taiyuan	太淵
tinnitus	KI 3	Taixi	太谿
weak knees	KI 3	Taixi	太谿
weak low back	KI 3	Taixi	太谿
wheezing	LU 9	Taiyuan	太淵

CHAPTER FOUR

All about the pain

The brain is in the brain, not on the site where one feels the pain. Once we learn how the pain mechanism works, we can manage the pain better.

4-1. Understanding the pain

Most of the chronic pain sufferers may not have a clear understanding of their pain and just want pain to go away.
Is this a physical pain or an emotional pain?
Is this an emotional pain that turned into a physical pain?
Where and why this pain is coming from?
Is this pain something that resting and relaxation can resolve?
Should I tolerate until the pain goes away, or need professional help?
Are there any other resources that I have not tried yet that might help?
I have tried everything and what should I do now? Am I hopeless? Should I learn to live with it?

If it is a chronic pain that lasted more than six weeks, the chances are it will not go away easily unless the proper treatment plan is implemented.
Yes, there is hope and there is something you can do to help yourself.

I had a patient in his sixties who had been suffering fibromyalgia for years. Every joint in his body was in pain; the pain in his left leg was unbearable due to poor circulation. A doctor even suggested amputating his leg. He tried everything. It seemed to him that his life was over. He stopped coming to see me.
A year and half later I ran into him at a shopping mall. He was so

happy to see me and wanted to show me how well he was doing. Miraculously, he looked like a new man. He told me that he did not have any pain or restriction of movement at all. He still had both legs. He was like a child jumping around, showing off . I asked him, "What did you do?" He answered, "I found the secret, and I did unwind myself."

He realized how tense his body was due to all the accumulated mental and physical stress. He decided to loosen up his body from head to toe by doing massage. He slowly gained his health back and all the pain was gone.

4-2. **Types of Pain**

Pain manifests in many different ways.

Referred Pain

This is defined as pain that is felt at a place in the body different from the injured or diseased part where the pain would be expected; such "angina pectoris can cause referred pain in the left shoulder", and "pain in the right shoulder can be referred pain from gallbladder disease".
Sometimes the brain cannot determine the specific source of the pain due to crisscross of the nervous signals. Referred pain can happen when nerve fibers from regions of high sensory input (such as the skin) and nerve fibers from regions of normally low sensory input (such as the internal organs) happen to converge on the same levels of the spinal cord.

Trigger Points

Trigger points or trigger sites are described as hyperirritable spots in skeletal muscle that are associated with palpable nodules in taut bands of muscle fibers. Trigger points are believed to be a common cause of pain.

There is no consistent methodology for diagnosis of trigger points and how they arise and why they produce specific patterns of referred pain. . The pain is often described as spreading or radiating. In addition, the referred pain is felt not at the site of the trigger-point origin, but remote from it.

Chronic Pain

Pain continues long after its cause is gone. When it lasts for 3 to 6 months or more, it is called chronic pain.

When the pain modulating system in the brain gets overloaded, the pain excitatory response out performs the pain inhibitory response. And this creates chronic pain. The hyperactive pain excitatory response can be triggered by many different factors such as fear and pain memory.

Spontaneous Pain

Pain is a burning or sharp stabbing/shooting pain that can occur spontaneously after nerve injury. The spontaneous pain is defined as neuropathic pain in the absence of any apparent stimulation. Damage of peripheral nerves sometimes accompanies excruciating pain that persist after the tissues have healed and the nerve fibers have regenerated. The cause appears to be inflammation within the nerves or tissues, caused by dying or degeneration of the injured nerve fibers within the same nerve. These pains may occur spontaneously for no apparent reason.

Reflex Sympathetic Dystrophy Syndrome (RSDS)
This is a condition that features a group of typical symptoms, including pain (often "burning" type), tenderness, and swelling of an extremity associated with varying degrees of sweating, warmth and/or coolness, flushing, discoloration, and shiny skin. The exact mechanism of how RSDS develops is not understood. The theories include irritation and abnormal excitation of nervous tissue, leading to abnormal impulses along nerves that affect blood vessels and skin.

Neuralgia
Trigeminal neuralgia and post-herpetic neuralgia is caused by peripheral nerve damage by viral infection, diabetes, and poor circulation.

Phantom pain
Perception of pain that an individual experiences relating to a limb or an organ that is not physically part of the body. Phantom limb pain is the feeling of pain in an absent limb or a portion of a limb.

Emotional pain
Sadness, depression, guilt, anxiety, fear, unexpressed anger when these emotions continues on for a prolonged period of time, this causes suffering within us. This produces a painful inner contraction, which ranges from annoying discomfort and severe physical and/or mental disease.

Emotionally induced physical pain

Change in mood or emotion, comes changes in every part of our body - physically, chemically, and functionally.
Common locations of stress referral pain: Low back/groin, Knee, Shoulder/scapula, Neck, Headaches, or Chest pain.

Aging pain

We often view pain as an inevitable part of the aging process, giving remarks such as "What do you expect? You're just getting older."

Are they right? No.
Epidemiological studies suggest that the prevalence of musculoskeletal pain generally declines with advancing age,19 and a study of patients in their last 2 years of life found pain to be inversely correlated with age.20 These findings refute the stereotype that advancing age inexorably involves pain, and challenge the notion that pain in later life is normal and expected, and unworthy of treatment.

Age-related pain progression is neither universal nor expected— and contradicts a purely biological paradigm in which pain inevitably worsens over time.

4-3. Pain Medications

a. NSAIDs (Non-Steroidal Anti-Inflammatory Drugs)
NSAIDs are drugs with analgesic and antipyretic (fever-reducing) effects and which have, in higher doses, anti-inflammatory effects. The term "nonsteroidal" is used to distinguish these drugs from steroids, which, among a broad range of other effects, have a similar eicosanoid-depressing, anti-inflammatory action. As analgesics, NSAIDs are unusual in that they are non-narcotic. The

most prominent members of this group of drugs are aspirin, ibuprofen, and naproxen.

b. COX-2 Inhibitors

COX-2 selective inhibitor is a form of non-steroidal anti-inflammatory drug (NSAID) that directly targets COX-2, an enzyme responsible for inflammation and pain. Selectivity for COX-2 reduces the risk of peptic ulceration, and is the main feature of celecoxib (brand name Celebrex) and rofecoxib (brand name Vioxx). COX-2 selectivity does not seem to reduce other adverse effects of NSAIDs (most notably an increased risk of renal failure), and some results have shown an increase in the risk for heart attack, thrombosis and stroke by a relative increase in thromboxane. Rofecoxib was taken off the market in 2004 because of these concerns.

c. Narcotic Pain Medications

All narcotic agents have a dissociative effect that helps patients manage pain. It does not actually deaden the   pain, but works to dissociate patients from the pain. Narcotic agents are strong and potentially addictive forms of medication. Commonly used narcotics are Morphine, Codeine (e.g. Tylenol #3), Hydrocodone (e.g. Vicodin), Oxycodone (e.g. Percocet, Oxycontin).

d. Central Analgesics: Acetaminophen

Analgesic, antipyretic, derivative of acetanilide. It has weak anti-inflammatory properties and is used as a common analgesic, but may cause liver, blood cell, and kidney damage.

Although the exact mechanism through which acetaminophen exert its effects has yet to be fully determined, this agent probably acts by inhibiting prostaglandin synthesis in the central nervous system (CNS). Inhibition of prostaglandin synthesis in the CNS results in elevation of the pain threshold and lowering of the thermal set point in the hypothalamus.

These drugs do not work for everybody and they have side effects from the long-term use such as stomach bleeding, heart attack, stroke, nausea, renal failure, thrombosis, stroke, constipation, dizziness, headache, drowsiness, vomiting, and danger of addition with the narcotic drugs. These drugs do not have any healing effect. They just block the perception of pain. Therefore, the root cause of the pain is not taken care of by taking these drugs.

4-4. Mindful meditation **and Pain Management**

Quote from "Mindfulness meditation–based pain relief: a mechanistic account"

2016 Jun, Department of Neurobiology and Anatomy, Wake Forest University School of Medicine, Winston-Salem, North Carolina

Abstract

Pain is a multidimensional experience that involves sensory, cognitive, and affective factors. The constellation of interactions between these factors renders the treatment of chronic pain challenging and financially burdensome. Further, the widespread use of opioids to treat chronic pain has led to an opioid epidemic characterized by exponential growth in opioid misuse and addiction. The staggering statistics related to opioid use highlight the importance of developing, testing, and validating fast-acting nonpharmacological approaches to treat pain. Mindfulness meditation is a technique that has been found to significantly reduce pain in experimental and clinical settings. The present review delineates findings from recent studies demonstrating that mindfulness meditation significantly attenuates pain through multiple, unique mechanisms—an important consideration for the millions of chronic pain patients seeking narcotic-free, self-facilitated pain therapy."

We postulate that mindfulness meditation could be such a suitable narcotic-free pain therapy for a number of reasons: firstly, mindfulness-based meditation has repeatedly been found to significantly reduce chronic pain symptomologies; second, mindfulness meditation attenuates pain through multiple unique psychological and neural processes; and further, it has recently been demonstrated that mindfulness meditation is more effective in reducing pain than placebo and does not engage endogenously driven opioidergic systems to reduce pain.

The subjective experience of pain: the subjective evaluation of pain. That is, previous experiences, expectations, mood, conditioning, desires, sensitization/habituation, and other cognitive factors can dramatically amplify and/or attenuate pain.

For thousands of years, Buddhist monks have postulated that the practice of mindfulness meditation can significantly alter the subjective experience of pain. For instance, the ancient Buddhist text, the Sullatta Sutta (The Arrow), states that meditation practitioners have the ability to fully experience the sensory aspect of pain (first arrow), and to "let go" of the evaluation (second arrow) of pain.

 "...When touched with a feeling of pain, the ordinary uninstructed person sorrows, grieves, and laments, beats his breast, becomes distraught." So he feels two pains, physical and mental.
Just as if they were to shoot a man with an arrow and, right

afterward, were to shoot him with another one, so that he would feel the pains of two arrows." The Buddha

The health-promoting effects of meditation are most pronounced for pain and opioid addiction and misuse, stress, depression and anxiety. Some recent studies of fibromyalgia and chronic low back pain patients who received mindfulness training also see a similar decoupling of sensory and affective pain, such that pain intensity or frequency does not necessarily decrease, but coping with the pain does improve.

Pain relief produced by mindful meditation is associated with significant reductions in pain-related brain activation (posterior insula, parietal operculum) and activation in higher-order brain regions, such as the ACC (Anterior Cingulate Cortex), PFC (Prefrontal Cortex), and insula. Importantly, the PFC, insula, and ACC contain high concentrations of opioid receptors and are associated with producing analgesia through descending inhibitory systems.

Mindful meditation for pain relief can be compared to removing the second arrow.

4-5. let go and Surrender
 Emotionally triggered physical pain such as Tension Myositis syndrome (TMS) is hard to identify and treat. To treat this type of pain we have to learn to accept who we are and free ourselves from emotional traps. We do not need to reenact to the emotion whenever something triggers it.

After enduring pain for a long time, the mind identifies pain as a part of self. The mind recognizes pain as a self-identification. Unknowingly mind is holding on to pain just like any other self-identification. Do not think that pain has to be with you. Do not reinforce your pain mentality. People can live with minor degenerative joints without pain. After all, pain is not at the joint or muscle, it's in the head.

When we fight pain with pain drugs, we are not really healing it. Pain becomes more vicious. Patients need to increase the dosage of pain drugs, and may become pain drug addicts.
 Another way of dealing with chronic pain is to stop fighting against it. To eliminate the pain is to eliminate the fear which sufferer is trying to avoid. Accept the fear in its fullest extent by overcoming the fear. By accepting and experiencing the worst, we remove the fear of pain and the pain itself.

"Let go and surrender, just do It." is not easy.
It is awfully difficult to meditate when one has an excruciating pain in the body. Acupuncture treatment for pain is very effective and a person need not go through all the ritual of mindful meditation. Acupuncture treatment is not blocking the pain. It calms the mind and facilitates healing by opening the energy flow to heal.

CHAPTER FIVE

5-1. COMMONLY USED ACUPUNCTURE POINTS

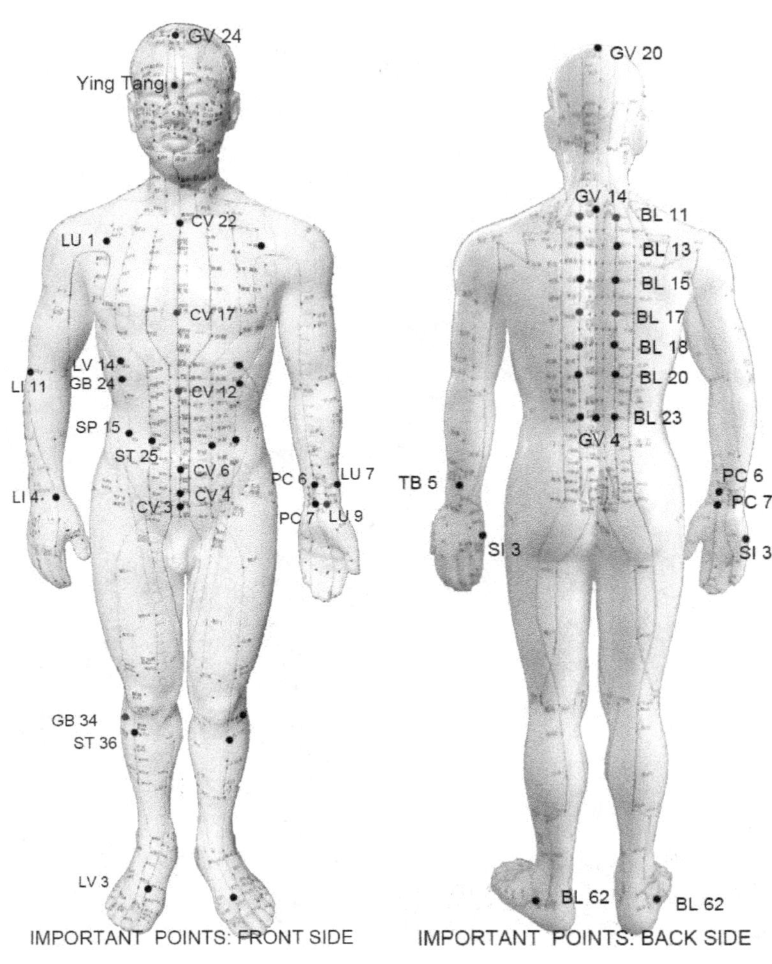

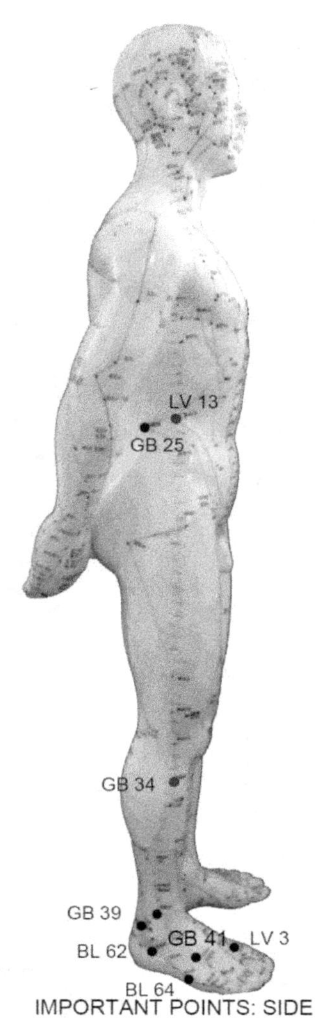

IMPORTANT POINTS: SIDE

Ying tang 印堂

Midway between the medial ends of the eyebrows.
Calms the spirit - insomnia, anxiety, stress.
Frontal headache.
Sinus issues - congestion, sinusitis.

SHEN TING 神庭 (GV 24)

0.5 cun above hairline in the center of the front hairline.
Frontal headache, dizziness, chronic sinusitis.
Anxiety, panic attacks

Bai hui 百會 (GV 20)

Midway on a line connecting the apex of both ears.
Headache, dizziness, eye pain and redness, stroke, hemiplegia, poor memory, tinnitus, blurred vision
Main point for prolapse, anal, uterine, vaginal, and for hemorrhoids.

Daz hui 大椎 (GV 14)

Below the spinous process of C7
Strengthening the neck and spine.
Colds and flu with fever and chills.
Spontaneous sweating

Shen dao 神道 (GV 11)

Below the spinous process of T5.
Palpitations, anxiety, poor memory, absent-mindedness, insomnia. Has strong effect on mind and mood.

Ming men 命門 (GV 4)

Below the spinous process of L2.
Low back pain, weak knees, nocturnal urination, impotence, menstrual disorders.
Adrenal exhaustion from stress or overwork, fatigue.

Zong ji 中極 (CV 3)

1 cun above CV 2 (pubic symphysis).
Urinary disorders: cystitis, dark/burning/urgent/frequent urination.
Dysmenorrhea, amenorrhea, fibroids, leukorrhea, uterine bleeding, uterine prolapse.
Genital itching, rashes, genital herpes, impotence.

Guan yuan 關元 (CV 4)

2 cun above CV 2 (pubic symphysis).
Main point for tonifying Qi: exhaustion, weakness, chronic fatigue.
Genito-urinary issues: incontinence, clear copious urine, nocturia.
Menstrual disorders: scanty menstruation, pale blood.
Sexual Issues: infertility, impotence, amenorrhea.

Qi hai 氣海 (CV 6)

1.5 cun below CV 8 (umbilicus).
Generally, useful for Qi tonification: weakness of the muscles and body generally.
Women's health: irregular menstruation, dysmenorrhea (painful menstruation / cramps), amenorrhea, leukorrhea.
Men's health – impotence, nighttime urination, hernia.

Deficiencies of the lower and middle warmers - abdominal distention, bloating, edema, poor digestion, loose stools, diarrhea, fatigue.

Zhong wan 中 脘 (CV 12)

4 cun above CV 8 (umbilicus)
All digestive issues - pain, bloating, reflux, vomiting, diarrhea.

Ju que 巨闕 (CV 14)

6 cun above CV 8 (umbilicus).
Mu Point of the Heart: pain/tightness in the Heart area.
Nausea, reflux, acid regurgitation, vomiting, abdominal or epigastric pain.
Shen (Spirit) disturbances: manic depression, mud, anger, poor memory, anxiety, palpitations, panic attacks, epilepsy.

Tan zong 膻中 (CV 17)

Level with the 4th ICS, midway between the nipples.
Main point for tonification of the upper warmer.
Tonify and move the Qi of the body.
Chronic lung issues: cough, asthma, Shortness of breath.

Tian tu 天突 (CV 22)

At the notch in the superior aspect of the suprasternal fossa.
All throat/vocal cord disorders: sore/dry throat, hoarseness, swallowing issues, speech issues such as loss of voice.
Upper chest Qi/Stagnation issues: asthma, wheezing, pain in the upper chest, tightness, oppression.

Fei shu 肺俞 (BL 13)
1.5 cun lateral to GV12 level with the spinous process of T3.
Main point for all Lung related issues: cough, asthma, bronchitis, sore throat, nasal congestion, shortness of breath.

Xin shu 心俞 (BL 15)
1.5 cun lateral to GV11 level with the spinous process of T5.
Main point for all heart related issues.
Emotional issues: palpitations, anxiety, easily frightened, stress, poor memory, Insomnia
Night sweats

Gan shu 肝俞 (BL 18)

1.5 cun lateral to GV 8 level with the spinous process of T9.
Main point for all Liver related condition: hepatitis, jaundice, cirrhosis.
Generalized blood stagnation, Qi stagnation.
Eye problems: pain, itching, dryness, redness, blurred vision, visual dizziness, twitching, night blindness.
Anger, depression, irritability, frustration, stress a/or PMS.
Hypochondriac and subcostal pain/distention.

Pi shu 脾俞 (BL 20)

1.5 cun lateral to GV 6 level with the spinous process of T11
Main point for all Spleen problems: abdominal pain, bloating, poor appetite, dysentery.
Blood related conditions - heavy menstrual bleeding, uterine bleeding.

Shen shu 腎俞 (BL23)

1.5 cun lateral to GV 4, level with L2.
Male deficiency related sexual problems: impotence.
Female sexual and reproductive disorders: irregular cycles, dysmenorrhea, amenorrhea, infertility, leukorrhea.
Tonification point in deficiency conditions: exhaustion, weakness, chronic fatigue.
Main point for acute or chronic low back pain.
Useful for water metabolism issues: edema, fluid retentions.

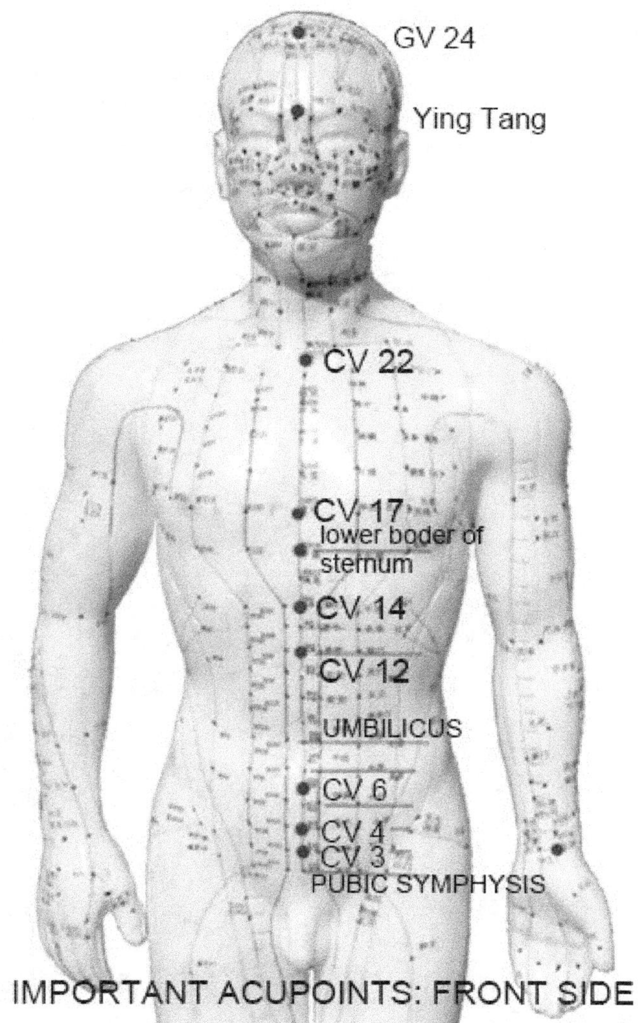
GV 24
Ying Tang
CV 22
CV 17
lower boder of
sternum
CV 14
CV 12
UMBILICUS
CV 6
CV 4
CV 3
PUBIC SYMPHYSIS
IMPORTANT ACUPOINTS: FRONT SIDE

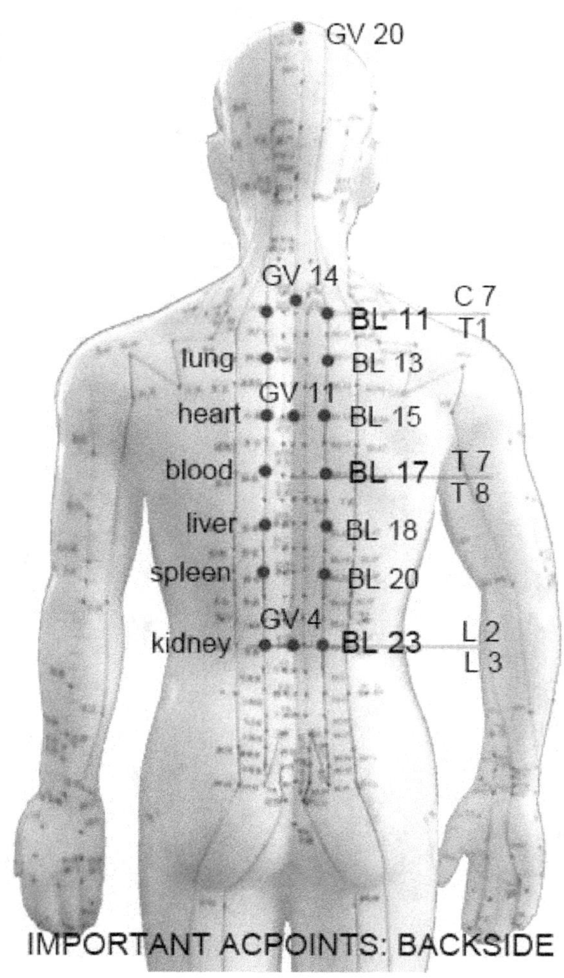

GV 20
GV 14
BL 11
C 7
T 1
lung
BL 13
GV 11
heart
BL 15
blood
BL 17
T 7
T 8
liver
BL 18
spleen
BL 20
GV 4
kidney
BL 23
L 2
L 3
IMPORTANT ACPOINTS: BACKSIDE

Shen mai 申脈 (BL 62)

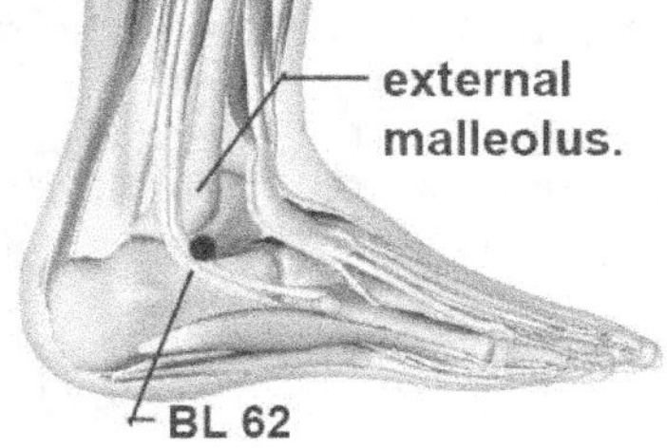

In a depression directly below the external malleolus.
With SI 3 for **low back pain**, difficulty walking, stiff neck or shoulders, occipital headache.

Zhong fu 中府 (LU 1)

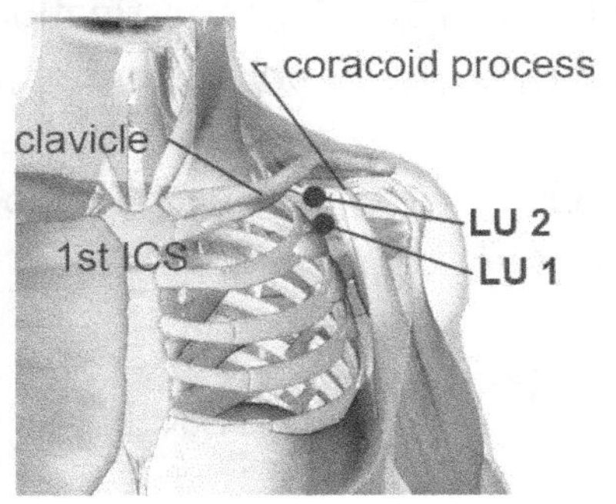

6 cun lateral to the anterior midline, level with the 1st ICS (intercostal space).
Lung Front MU Point, useful for all Lung issues: cough, wheezing, **asthma**.

Lie que 列缺(LU 7)

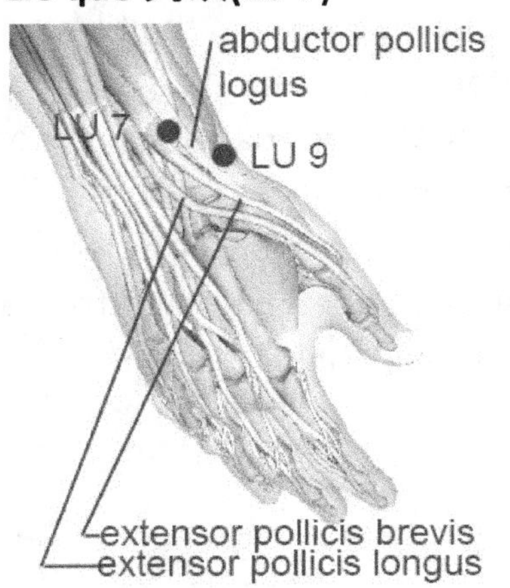

1.5 cun above the transverse crease of the wrist, superior to the styloid process of the radius.
As Master Point of the CV (Conception, Ren Mai), paired with KI 6 of the Yin Qiao Mai, it treats genitourinary and gynecological issues.
Exterior Wind: runny nose, scratchy throat, sneezing.
Command Point of the **Head and neck: headache**, Bell's palsy.
Pain of the thumb.

Tai yuan 太淵 (LU 9)

On transverse crease of the wrist on the lateral side of the radial artery.
Tonify Lung Qi: cough asthma, wheezing, shortness of breath.
Wrist pain

Tian shu 天樞 (ST 25)

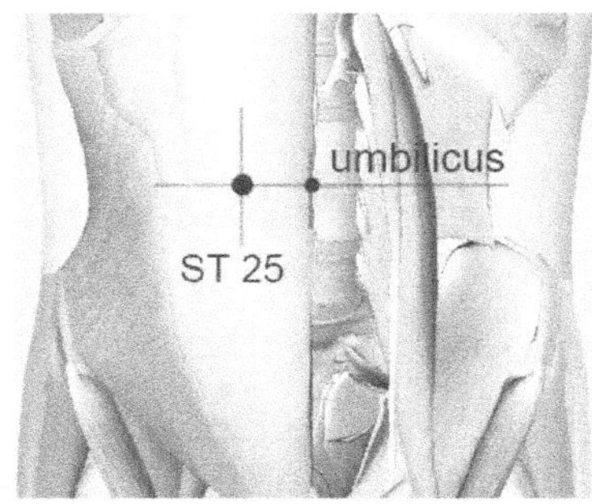

2 cun lateral to the midline, lateral to CV8 at the level of the umbilicus.
All intestinal issues: constipation, diarrhea, dysentery, distention, pain.
Infertility, irregular menstruation.
Mu Point of Large Intestine.

Zu san li 足三里 (ST 36)

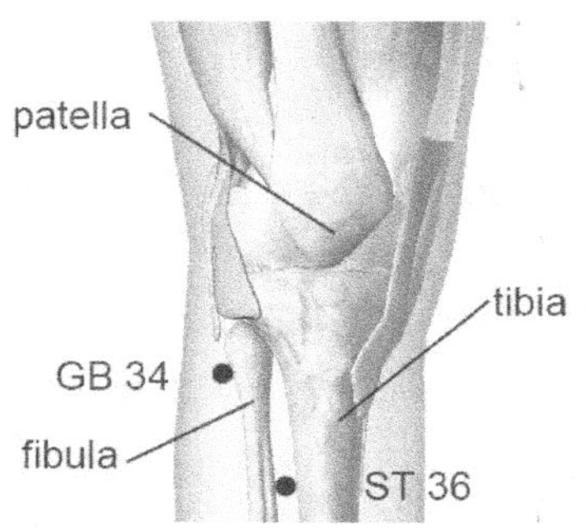

3 cun below the patella, one finger width lateral from the anterior crest of the tibia, in the tibialis anterior muscle.
Tonify Qi: poor digestion, general weakness.
The Stomach a/or the Spleen issues: abdominal/epigastric pain, borborygmus, bloating, nausea, vomiting, GERD, hiccups, diarrhea, constipation, etc.
Lower leg pain.

Gong sun 公孫 (SP 4)

On the medial aspect of the foot, in the depression distal and inferior to the base of the first metatarsal bone.
The Stomach and Intestines issues: abdominal or epigastric pain,

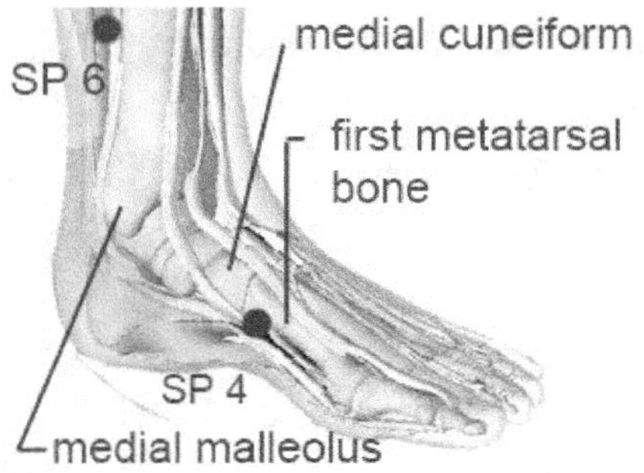

dysentery.

Gynecological issues: masses, fibroids, cysts, irregular menstruation.

With PC 6 for chest and heart pain, Shen disorders, anxiety, insomnia, nervousness.

San yin jiao 三陰交(SP 6)

3 cun directly above the tip of the medial malleolus on the posterior border of the tibia.

Tonify Yin and Blood, Liver, Kidney.

Digestive disorders

Gynecological issues, male sexual issues

Menstrual issues: irregular, amenorrhea, dysmenorrhea.

Bleeding disorders, uterine bleeding

Tai chong 太沖 (LV 3)

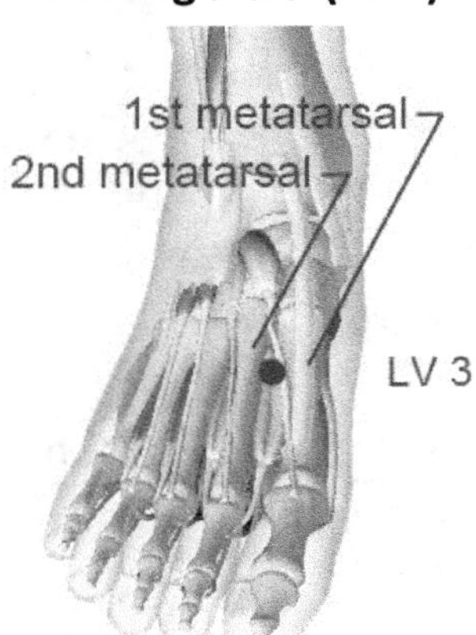

On the dorsum of the foot in a depression distal to the junctions of the 1st and 2nd metatarsal bones.

Generally, resolves stagnation and tonifies Yin - balancing for all Liver pathologies.

Liver Qi Stagnation / Liver Yang Rising: headaches, dizziness.

Menstrual issues: dysmenorrhea, amenorrhea, PMS, breast tenderness.

Genital issues: pain/swelling, hernia, impotence,
Stagnation in the middle Burner: subcostal tension, chest/flank pain, swellings in the axillary region.

Digestive issues: nausea, vomiting, constipation, diarrhea.
Calming point - anger, irritability, insomnia, anxiety.
With LI 4, four gates treatment - powerfully affects the flow of Qi and Blood in the body.

Zhang men 章門 (LV 13)

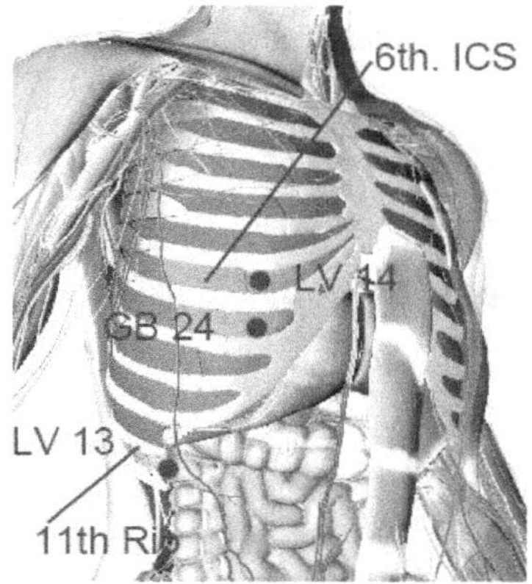

On the lateral side of the abdomen below the free end of the 11th rib. Pain and distention of the abdomen, vomiting, constipation, diarrhea, bloating.

Qi men 期門 (LV 14)

Directly below the nipple, 4 cun lateral to the midline in the 6th intercostal groove.

Effects Liver, Qi/Blood stagnation: hepatitis, gallstones. Emotional imbalances: anger, irritability.

Shen men 神門(HT 7)

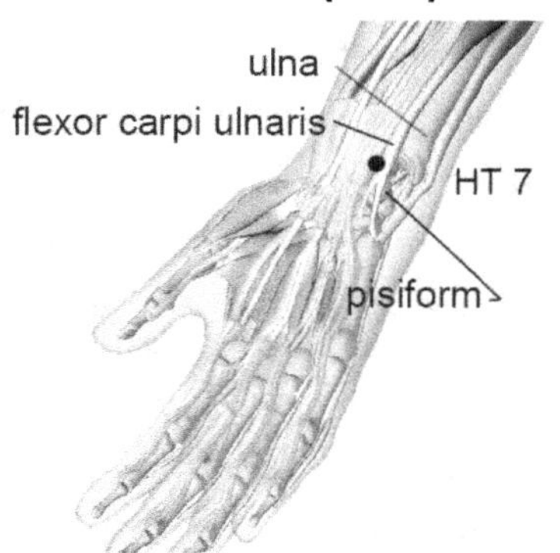

On the ulnar end of the transverse crease of the wrist, in the small depression between the pisiform and ulna bones, on the radial side of the flexor carpi ulnaris tendon.
Emotional issues: insomnia, anxiety, mania, anxiety w/palpitations, nausea, or fear.

Heart palpitations, irregular heartbeat, pounding heart, angina.

Nei guan 內關 (PC 6)

2 cun above the wrist crease between the tendons of palmaris longus and flexor carpi radialis.

Opens and relaxes the chest, chest tightness, asthma, angina, palpitations.

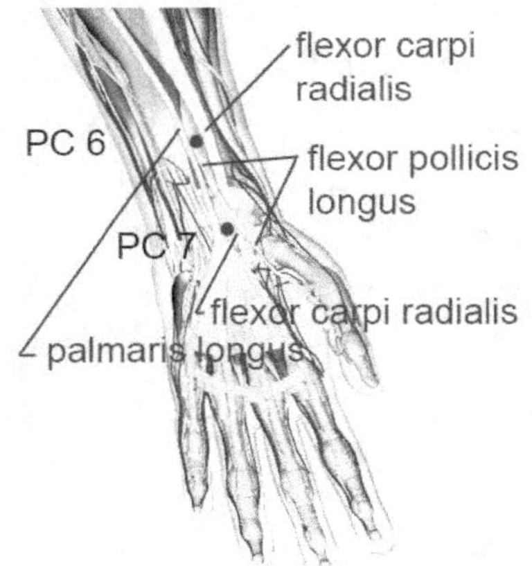

Insomnia, mania, nervousness, stress, poor memory.
Nausea, **seasickness, motion sickness,** vomiting, epigastric pain.
Carpal Tunnel Syndrome.

Da ling 大陵**(PC 7)**

In the middle of the transverse crease of the wrist, between the tendons of m. palmaris longus and m. flexor carpi radialis.

Cardiac pain, palpitation, pain in the chest and hypochondrium
Gastric pain, vomiting
Manic psychosis, **Carpal Tunnel Syndrome**

Zhao hai 照海**(KI 6)**

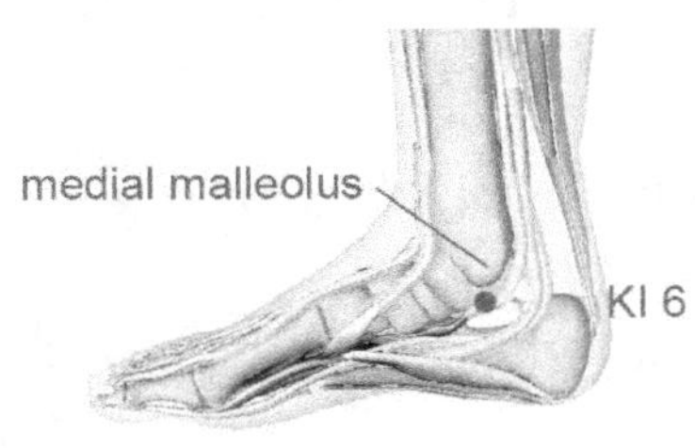

In a depression below the tip of the medial malleolus.
Dizziness. Tinnitus. Night sweating. Backache. Dry and red eyes. Blurred vision. Floater.
Pain, stress and strain of the muscles of the legs. Cramp in lower limb.
Menstrual issues: amenorrhea, dysmenorrhea, infertility.
Insomnia, disturbed sleep, yin deficient symptoms such as hot hands/feet, night sweats.
Anxiety disorders, fear, fright.

He gu 合谷 **(LI 4)**

On the dorsum of the hand, between the 1st and 2nd metacarpal bones.

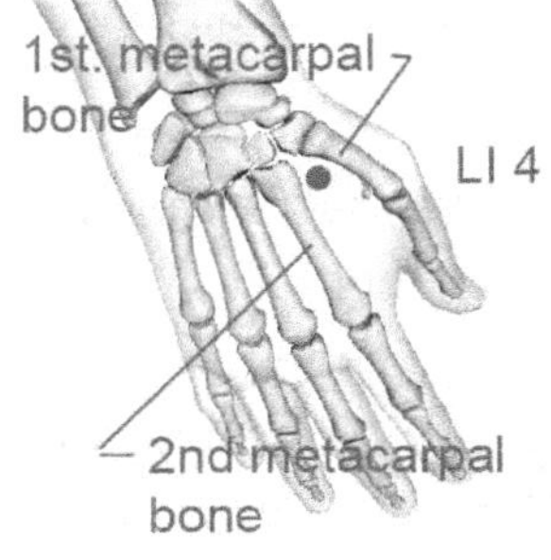

Releases the exterior for wind-cold or wind-heat syndromes

Strengthens the Wei (protective) Qi, improves immunity

Any problem on the face: mouth, teeth, jaw, toothache, allergies, rhinitis, hay fever, acne, eye problems, etc.

Headache, especially frontal, sinusitis

Chronic pain: use the four gates, LI 4 & LV 3 to strongly move the Qi and Blood in the body clearing stagnation and alleviating pain.

Que chi 曲池 (LI 11)

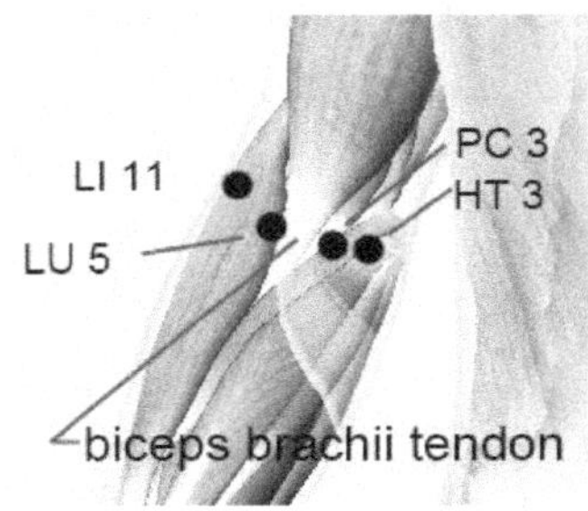

With a bent elbow, the point lies in the depression at the lateral end of the transverse cubital crease, midway between LU5 and the lateral epicondyle of the humerus. (LU5 Chize: On the cubital crease, in the depression lateral to biceps brachii tendon.)

Reduction of high fevers.

Skin disorder: red, itchy, oozing, inflamed (hives, herpes zoster, acne).

Elbow and upper limb disorders, pain and inflammation, atrophy,

Hou xi 後溪(SI 3)

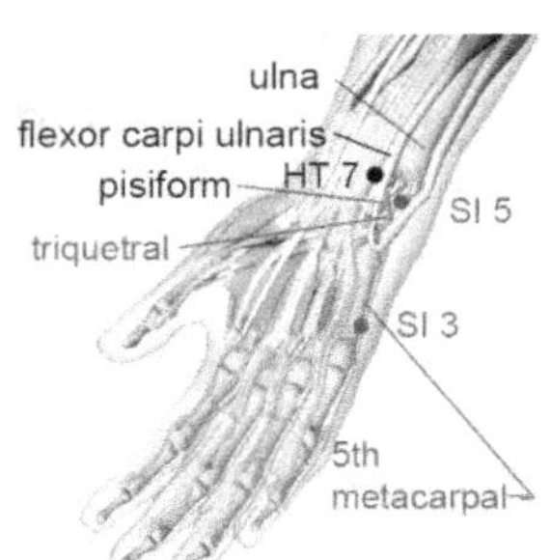

With a loose fist made, In the depression proximal to the head of the fifth metacarpal bone, at the junction of the red and white skin.

Master Point of the GV (Du Mai, Governing Vessel).

Pain: hand, arm, neck, scapula, back.

Occipital headache

Clears heat from the head, ears and eyes, eye redness,

inflammation, visual dizziness, earache, tinnitus, sore throat.
Calms the spirit, anxiety, manic depression.

Wai guan 外關 (TB 5)

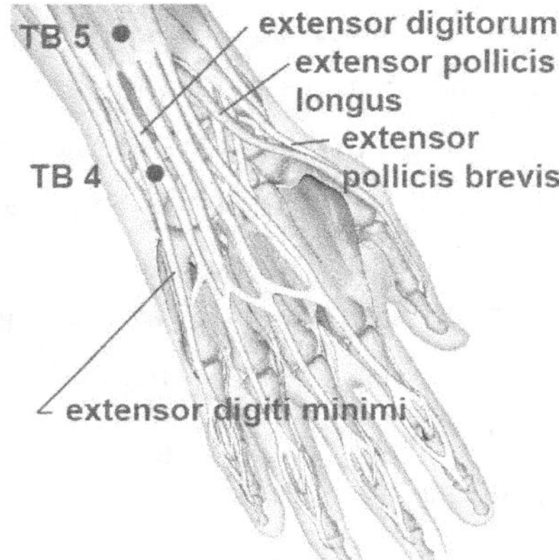

On the dorsum of the forearm, 2 cun above TW4 between the radius and the ulna. (**TB 4:** On the transverse crease of the dorsum of the wrist between the tendons of muscles extensor digitorum and extensor digiti minimi.)
Sedate for wind-heat, fever, common cold.
Headache, migraines with stiffness or pain in the posterior and lateral aspects of the neck.
Upper limb disorders including the elbow, forearm, wrist and hand.
Luo connecting point of the TB connects to the PC.
TB 5 & PC 6 as master points of the Yang Wei and Yin Wei respectively can affect the balance of yin and yang in the body.
If right pulse is stronger than the left (more Qi than Blood) disperse TB 5 & tonify PC 6, and vice versa

Ri yue 日月 (GB 24)

Directly below the nipple in the 7th intercostal space, inferior to LV 14.
Mu point of the Gallbladder.

Liver & Gallbladder issues: gallstones, hepatitis, jaundice.
Nausea, vomiting, sour belching, bitter taste, acid reflux.
Lithiasis (stones) in the Gallbladder.
Emotional imbalances: fearfulness, shyness, indecisiveness, timidity, sighing.

Jing men 京門 (GB 25)

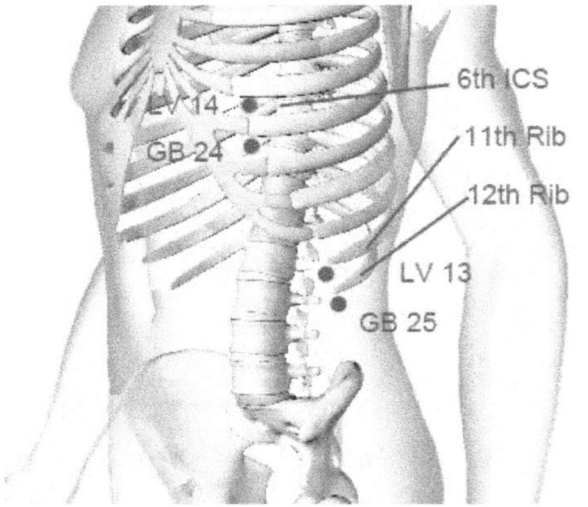

On the lateral side of the abdomen, at the lower border of the free end of the 12th rib.
Mu point of the Kidney. Regulates the waterway in the Lower Burner. Regulates Spleen and Intestines. Strengthens the lower back. Diuretic point - urinary retention, difficult urination, edema. Urinary tract stones: assists passage

Yang ling quan 陽陵泉 (GB 34)

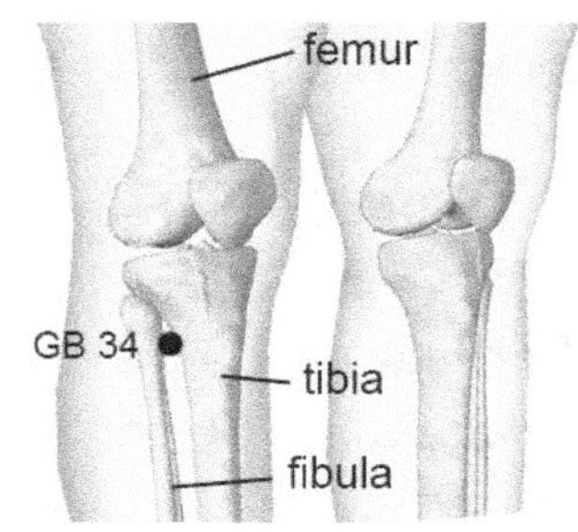

In a depression anterior and inferior to the head of the fibula.
Hui Meeting of the Sinews: useful for treating soft tissue issues: contracture, cramping, pain, spasm, weakness, numbness, paralysis. Lower He Sea of the GB: cholecystitis, hepatitis, jaundice, nausea, vomiting, bitter taste in mouth, gallstones.

Xuan zhong 懸鐘 (GB 39)

3 cun above the tip of the lateral malleolus in a depression between the posterior border of the fibula and the tendons of peroneous (fibularis) longus and brevis muscles.

Hui Meeting of the Marrow: the bone marrow, ligaments, tendons, muscles, bones issues (pain, spasms, numbness, weakness). Kidney Deficiency: thought to strengthen immunity.

Zu ling qi 足臨泣 (GB 41)

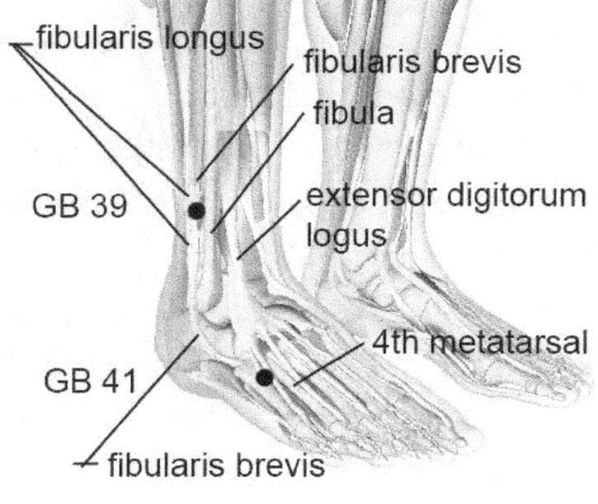

On the lateral side of the dorsum of the foot, proximal to the 4th metatarso-phalangeal joint, in the depression lateral to the tendon of m. extensor digitorum.

Moves Liver Qi: headaches, useful for eye problems, redness, swelling and,

tearing, excessive lacrimation.
Local point for lateral foot issues - pain, cramping

THE EIGHT INFLUENTIAL POINTS (八會穴)

The Eight Influential Points regulate the function of the zangfu organs, promote the circulation of qi and blood, support tendons and nourish marrow: Organs, Zang (臟), Fu 부(腑), Qi (氣), Blood (血), Bone (骨), Marrow (髓), Tendon (筋), Blood Vessel, Pulse (脈).

Zhang men 章門 (LV 13), the Influential Point of Zang organs.
Zhong Wan 中脘 (CV 12), the Influential Point of the fu organs.
Shan zhong 膻中 (CV 17), the Influential Point of Qi.
Ge shu 膈俞 (BL 17), the Influential Point of blood.
Yang ling quan 陽陵泉 (GB 34), the Influential Point of tendons.
Tai yuan 太淵 (LU 9), the Influential Point of the vessel/pulse.
Da shu 大杼 (BL 11), the Influential Point of the bones.
Xuan zhong 懸鐘 (GB 39), the Influential Point of the marrow.

Respective Influential Points can be selected for treating disorders associated with the above eight functional parts of the body with other acupuncture points.

Zhang men 章門 **(LV 13)** is the Influential Point of Zang organs and is also the Front-mu point of the spleen. This point can be used in the treatment of disorders of Zang organs, such as spleenomegaly, hepatomegaly, hypochondriac pain or jaundice.

Zhong Wan 中脘 **(CV 12)** is the Influential Point of the fu organs and is also the Front-mu point of the stomach.

Shan zhong 膻中 **(CV 17)** is the Influential Point of Qi. This point is in close proximity to the lung, the organ that dominates Qi. This point, also called Upper-Qihai, can be used for treating disorders , shortness of breath, asthma and hiccup.

Ge shu 膈俞 **(BL 17)** is the Influential Point of blood, being located between Xin shu (heart point) and Gan shu (liver point). It is used for treating disorders of blood such as anemia, stasis of blood.

Yang ling quan 陽陵泉 **(GB 34)** is the Influential Point of the tendons and is also the He-sea point of the Gallbladder Meridian. It is used for treating disorders such as spasm and painful tendons, numbness ,, or hemiplegia.

Tai yuan 太淵 **(LU 9)** is the Influential Point of vessels/pulse, also the Yuan (source) point of the Lung Meridian, is located at the wrist where the pulse is palpated. This point can be used for treating disorder of the vessels, such as vasculitis, acrotism (a lack or defect of the pulse) and arteriosclerosis.

Da shu 大杼 **(BL 11)** is the Influential Point of bones. This point is located superior to all of the Back-shu points. It can be used for treating disorders of the bones such as pain in the shoulder, scapula or back.

Xuan zhong 懸鐘 **(GB 39)** is the Influential Point of marrow.

Marrow is thought of helping the growth of bones. Thus, it is an essential factor in the ability to walk normally. It is used in the treatment of disorders of the marrow, such as myasthenia and anemia.

Clinically, the Influential Points can be used as main points or secondary points being prescribed according to the varying symptoms and signs.

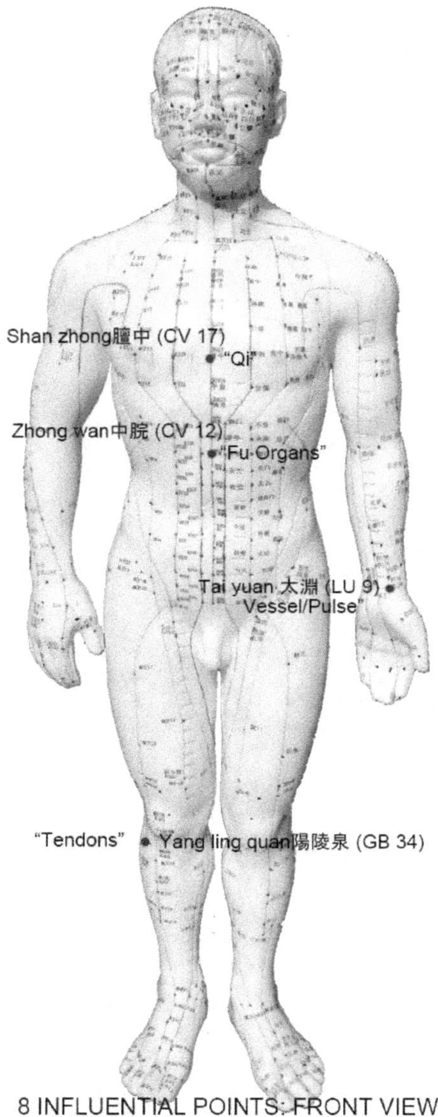

Shan zhong膻中 (CV 17)
"Qi"
Zhong wan中脘 (CV 12)
"Fu Organs"
Tai yuan 太淵 (LU 9)
Vessel/Pulse
"Tendons"
Yang ling quan陽陵泉 (GB 34)
8 INFLUENTIAL POINTS: FRONT VIEW

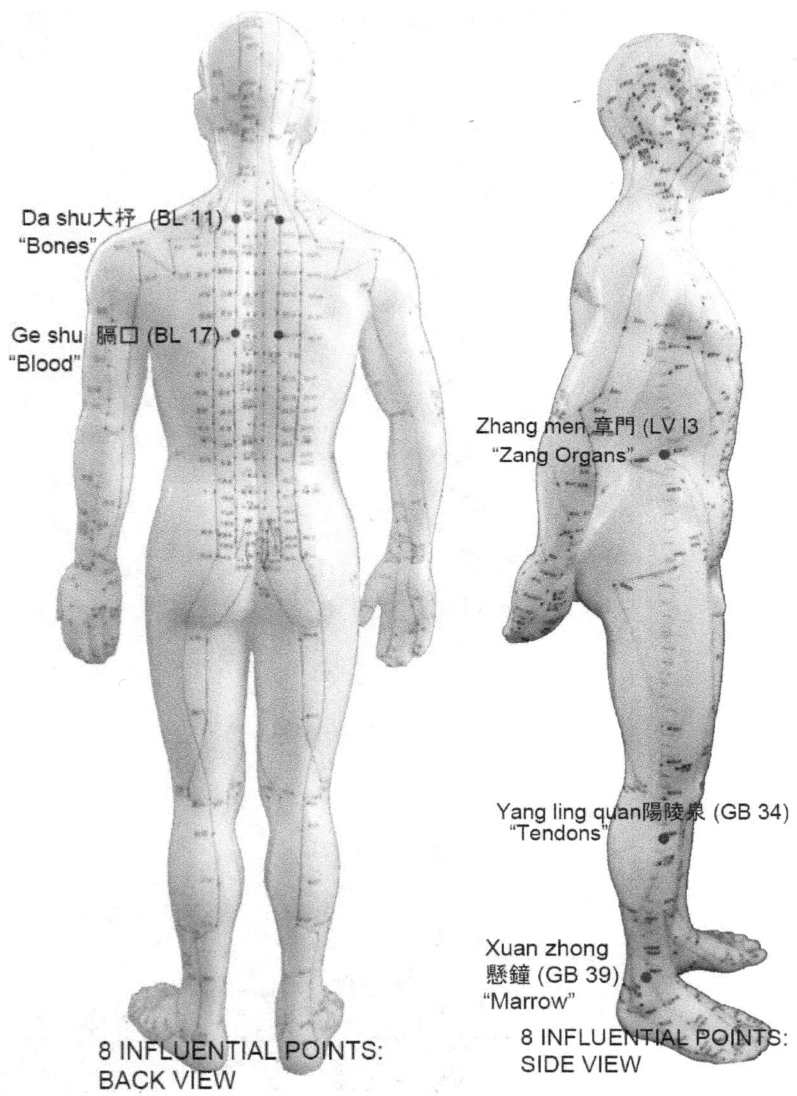

Da shu 大杼 (BL 11)
"Bones"
Ge shu 膈口 (BL 17)
"Blood"
Zhang men 章門 (LV l3)
"Zang Organs"
Yang ling quan 陽陵泉 (GB 34)
"Tendons"
Xuan zhong 懸鐘 (GB 39)
"Marrow"
8 INFLUENTIAL POINTS:
BACK VIEW
8 INFLUENTIAL POINTS:
SIDE VIEW

CHAPTER SIX

6-1. ACUPUNCTURE POINT LOCATION

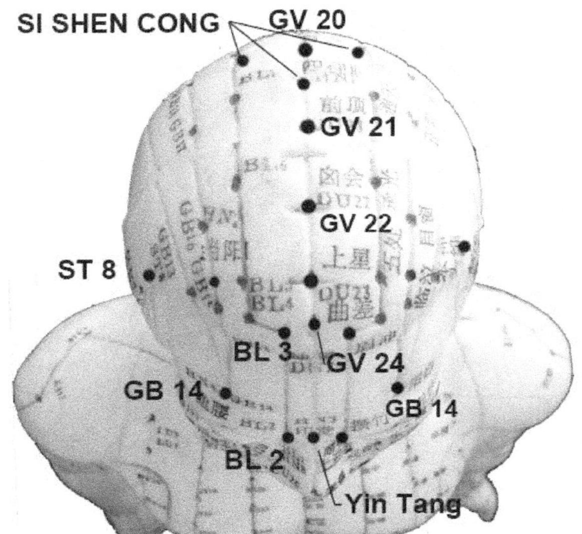

ACUPOINTS: HEAD

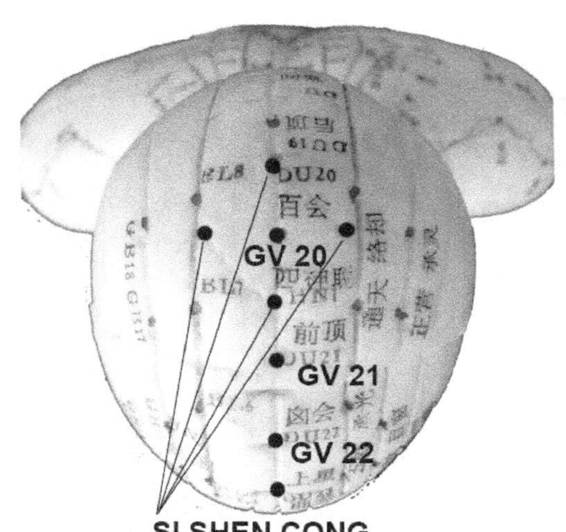

SI SHEN CONG

ACUPOINTS: TOP OF HEAD

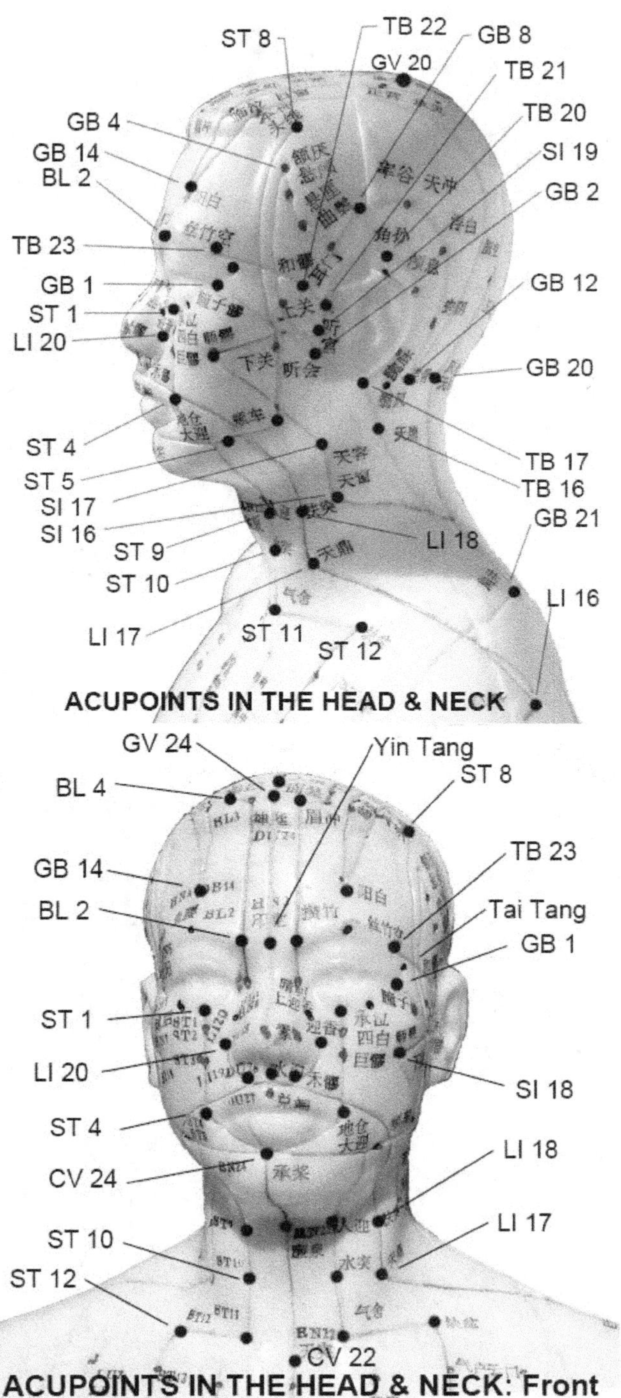

ST 8
TB 22
GB 8
GV 20
TB 21
TB 20
SI 19
GB 4
GB 14
BL 2
GB 2
TB 23
GB 12
GB 1
ST 1
LI 20
GB 20
ST 4
ST 5
SI 17
SI 16
TB 17
TB 16
GB 21
ST 9
ST 10
LI 18
LI 16
LI 17
ST 11
ST 12
ACUPOINTS IN THE HEAD & NECK
GV 24
Yin Tang
ST 8
BL 4
TB 23
GB 14
BL 2
Tai Tang
GB 1
ST 1
LI 20
SI 18
ST 4
CV 24
LI 18
ST 10
LI 17
ST 12
CV 22
ACUPOINTS IN THE HEAD & NECK: Front

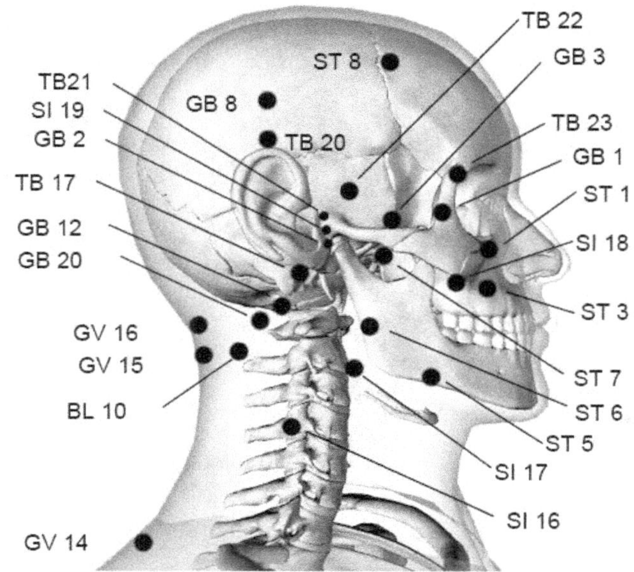

ACUPOINTS: HEAD, SIDE

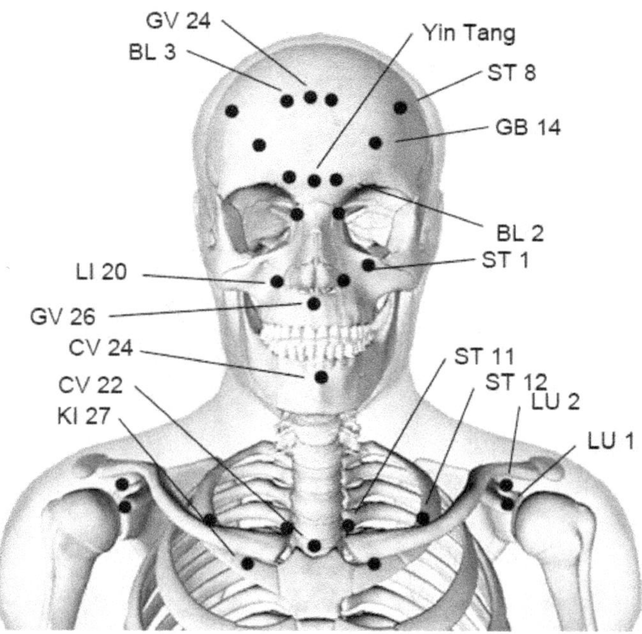

ACUPOINTS: FACE, FRONT

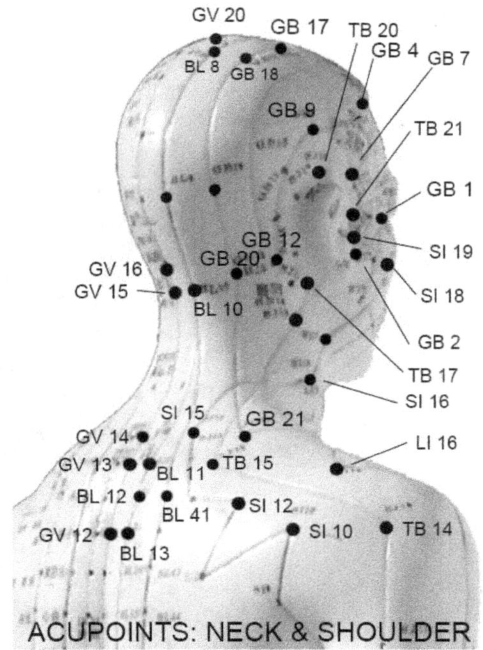

GV 20
GB 17
TB 20
GB 4
GB 7
BL 8
GB 18
GB 9
TB 21
GB 1
GB 12
SI 19
GV 16
GB 20
GV 15
SI 18
BL 10
GB 2
TB 17
SI 16
SI 15
GB 21
GV 14
LI 16
GV 13
BL 11
TB 15
BL 12
BL 41
SI 12
GV 12
SI 10
TB 14
BL 13
ACUPOINTS: NECK & SHOULDER

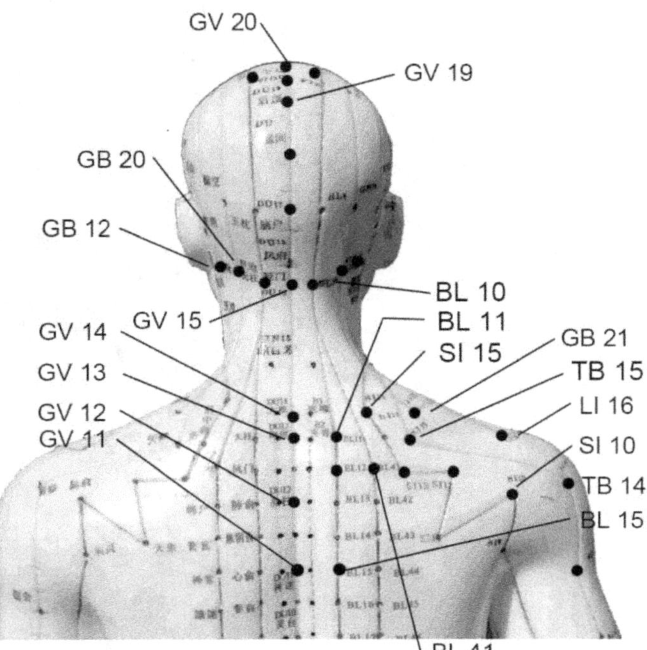

GV 20
GV 19
GB 20
GB 12
BL 10
BL 11
GV 14
SI 15
GB 21
GV 13
TB 15
GV 12
LI 16
GV 11
SI 10
TB 14
BL 15
BL 41
ACUPOINTS: UPPER BACK & HEAD

MERIDIANS: UPPER BODY

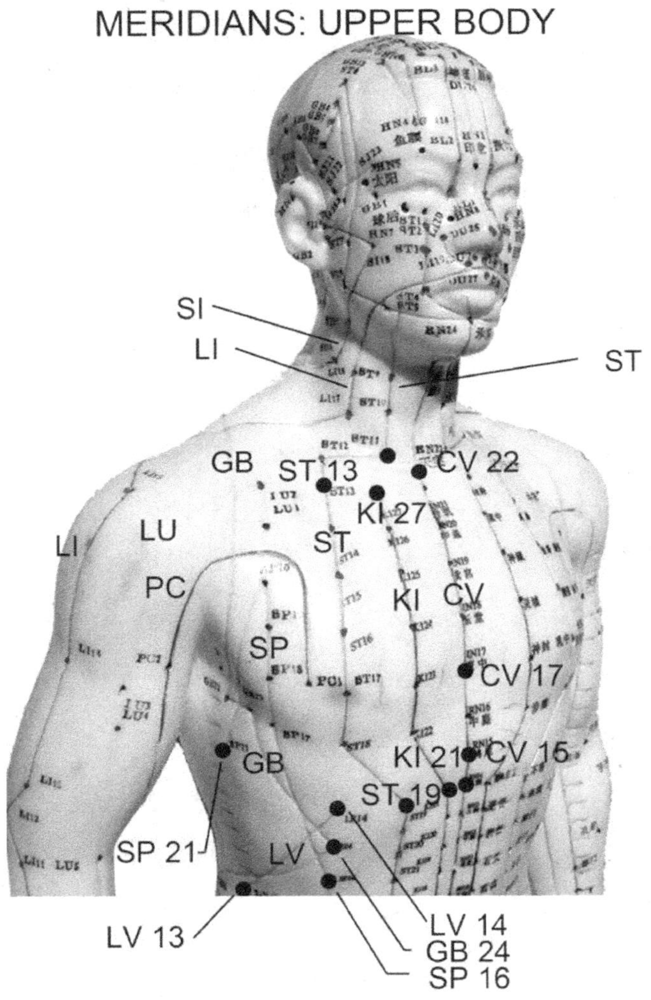

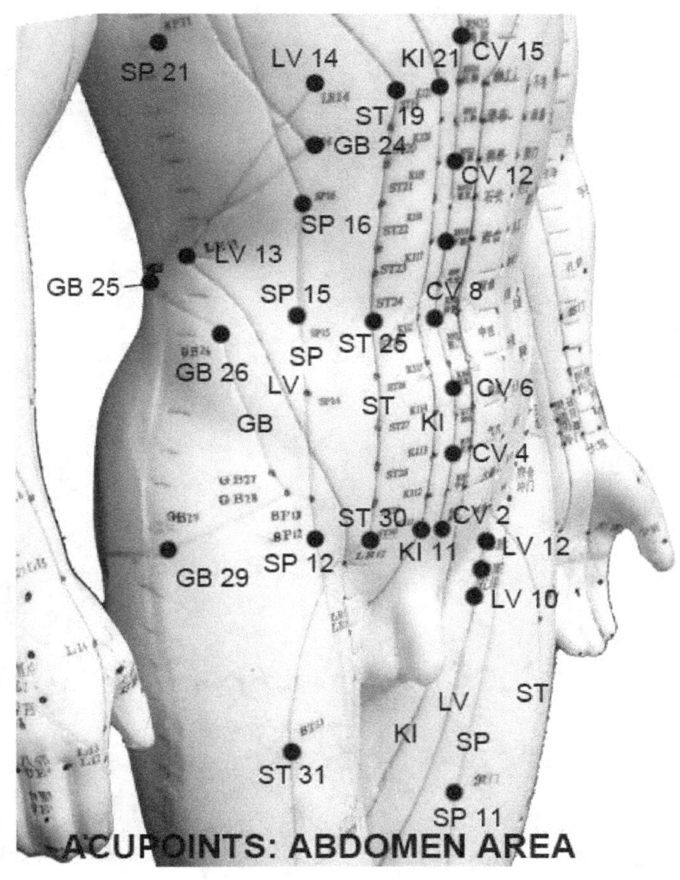

SP 21
LV 14
KI 21
CV 15
ST 19
GB 24
CV 12
SP 16
LV 13
GB 25
SP 15
CV 8
GB 26
SP
ST 25
LV
CV 6
GB
ST
KI
CV 4
GB 29
ST 30
CV 2
SP 12
KI 11
LV 12
LV 10
ST 31
KI
LV
SP
ST
SP 11
ACUPOINTS: ABDOMEN AREA

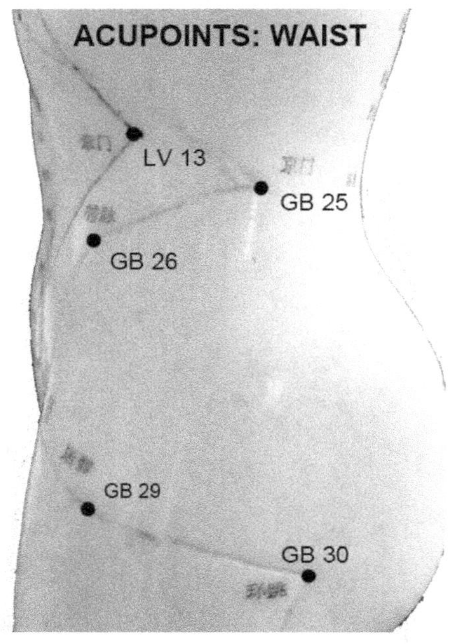

ACUPOINTS: WAIST
LV 13
GB 25
GB 26
GB 29
GB 30

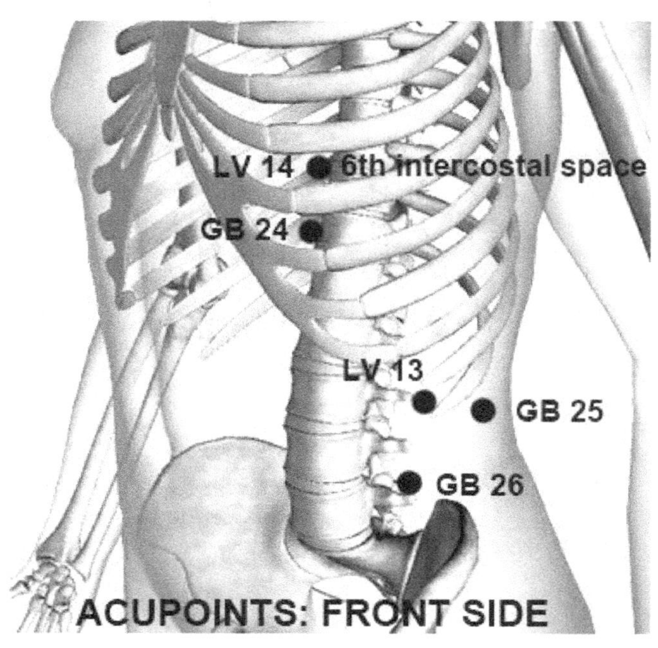

LV 14
6th intercostal space
GB 24
LV 13
GB 25
GB 26
ACUPOINTS: FRONT SIDE

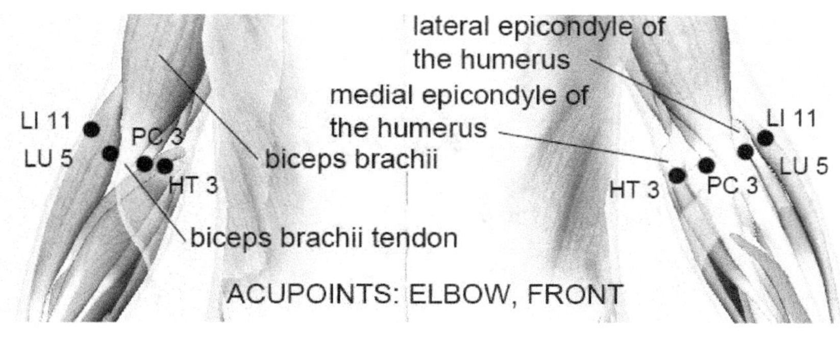
lateral epicondyle of
the humerus
medial epicondyle of
the humerus
biceps brachii
LI 11
LU 5
PC 3
HT 3
biceps brachii tendon
LI 11
LU 5
HT 3
PC 3
ACUPOINTS: ELBOW, FRONT

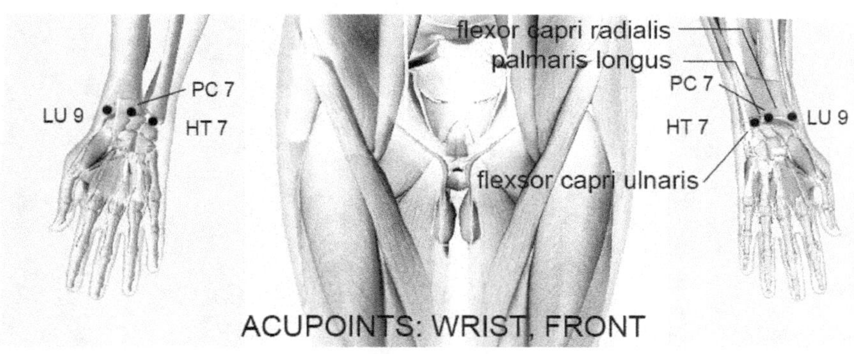
flexor capri radialis
palmaris longus
PC 7
LU 9
HT 7
PC 7
HT 7
LU 9
flexsor capri ulnaris
ACUPOINTS: WRIST, FRONT

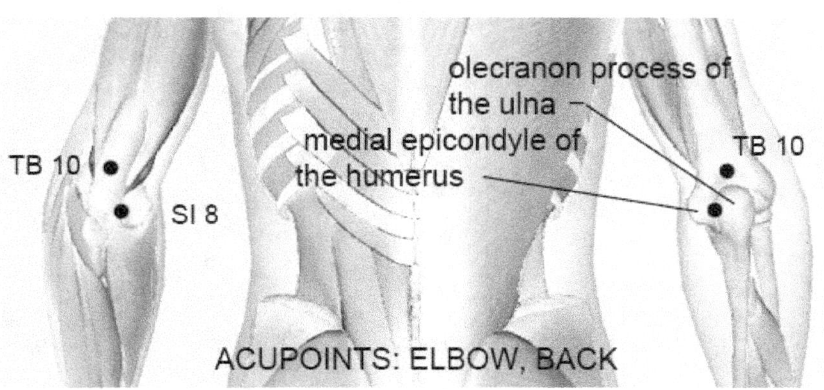
olecranon process of
the ulna
medial epicondyle of
the humerus
TB 10
TB 10
SI 8
ACUPOINTS: ELBOW, BACK

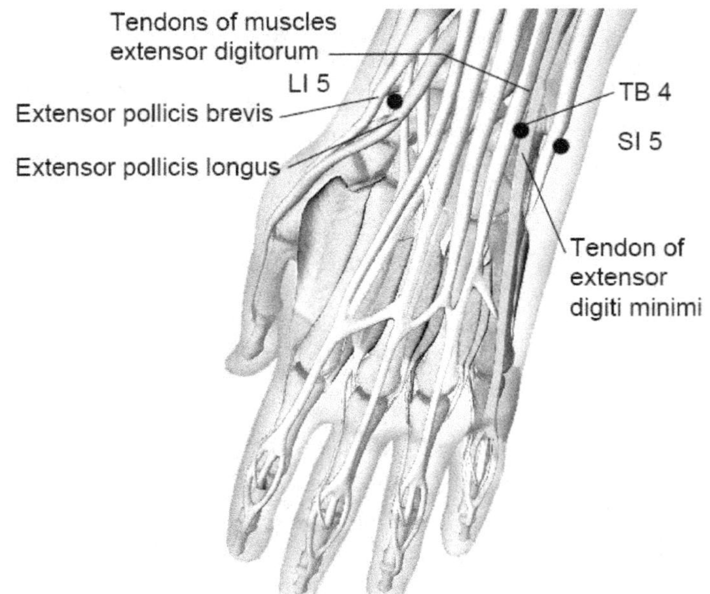

ACUPOINTS: WRIST, BACK

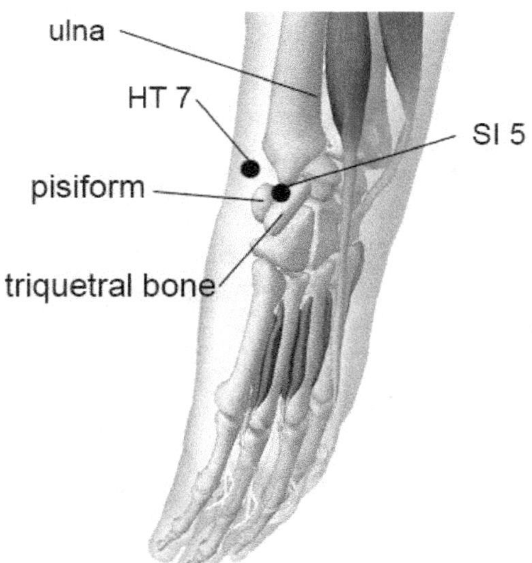

ACUPOINTS: HT 7, SI 5

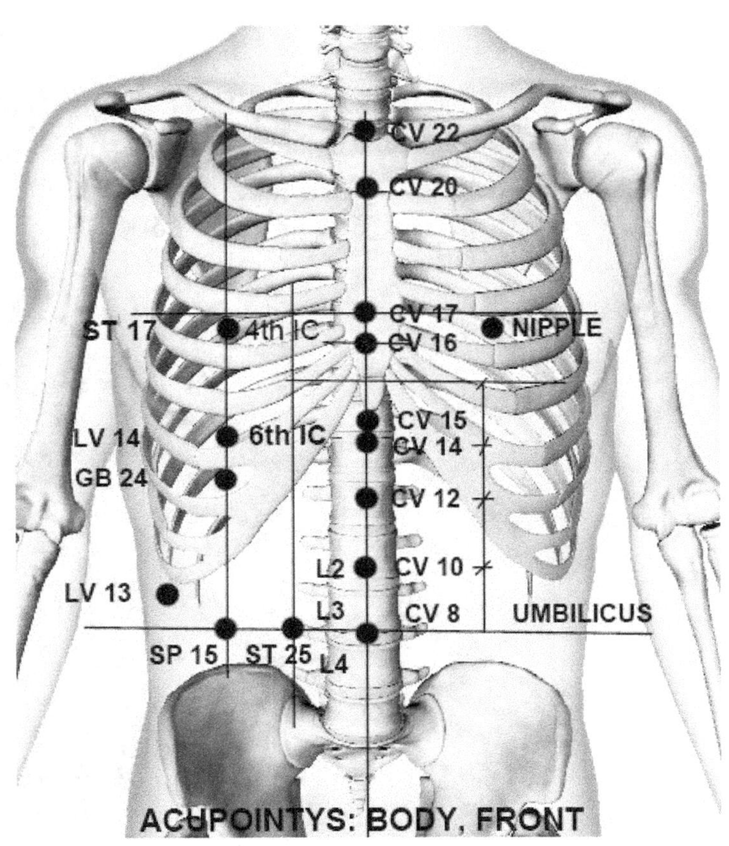

CV 22
CV 20
CV 17
ST 17
4th IC
NIPPLE
CV 16
CV 15
LV 14
6th IC
CV 14
GB 24
CV 12
CV 10
L2
LV 13
L3
CV 8
UMBILICUS
SP 15
ST 25
L4
ACUPOINTYS: BODY, FRONT

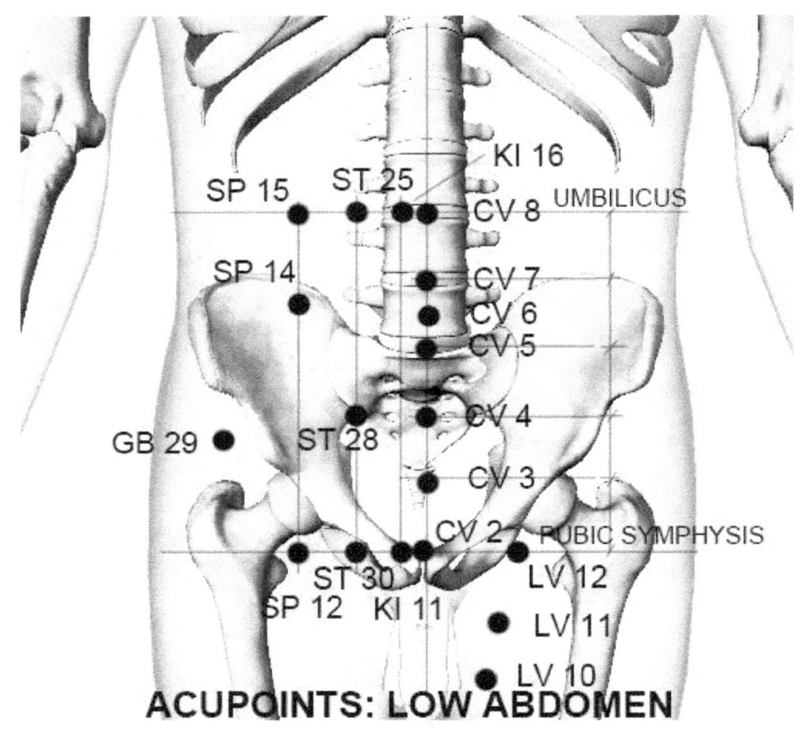

KI 16
SP 15
ST 25
CV 8
UMBILICUS
SP 14
CV 7
CV 6
CV 5
CV 4
GB 29
ST 28
CV 3
CV 2
PUBIC SYMPHYSIS
ST 30
LV 12
SP 12
KI 11
LV 11
LV 10
ACUPOINTS: LOW ABDOMEN

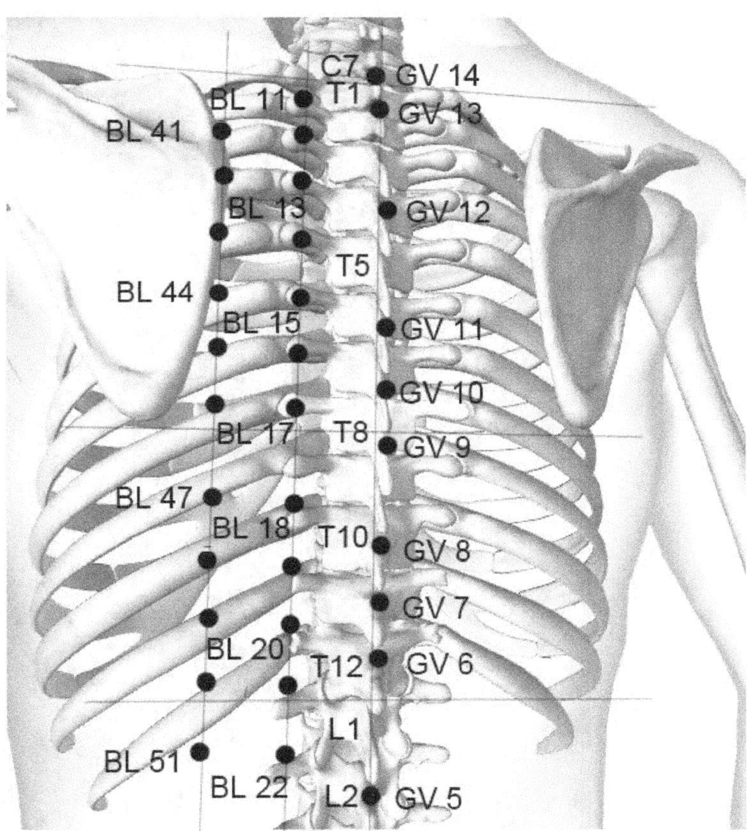

ACUPOINTS: BL, GV AT THORACIC AREA

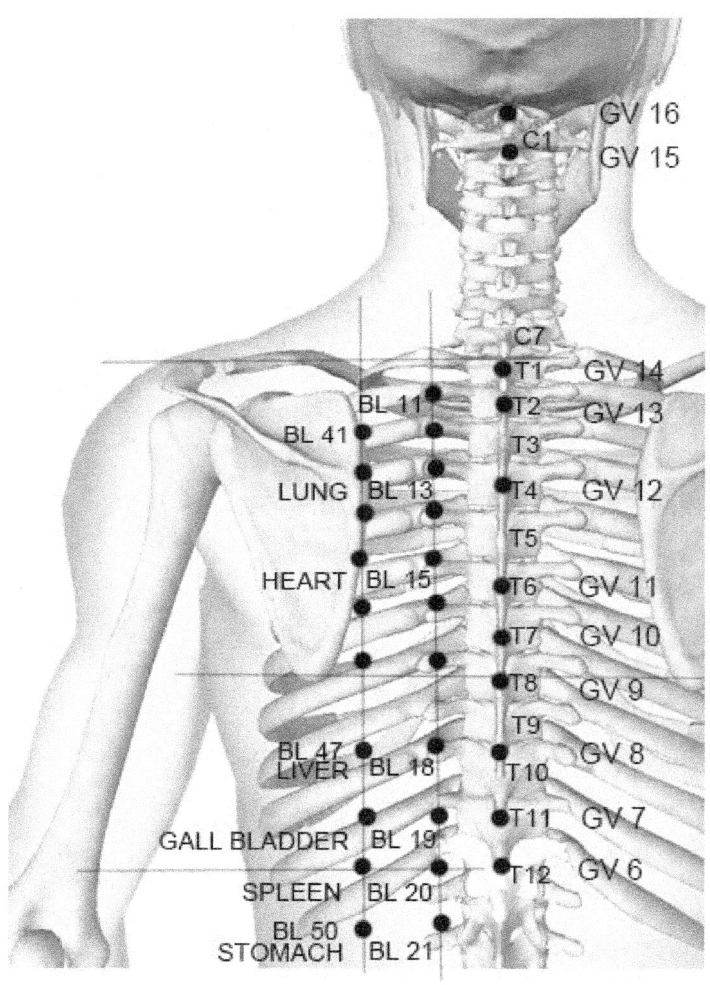

ACUPOINTS: BL, GV at THORACIC

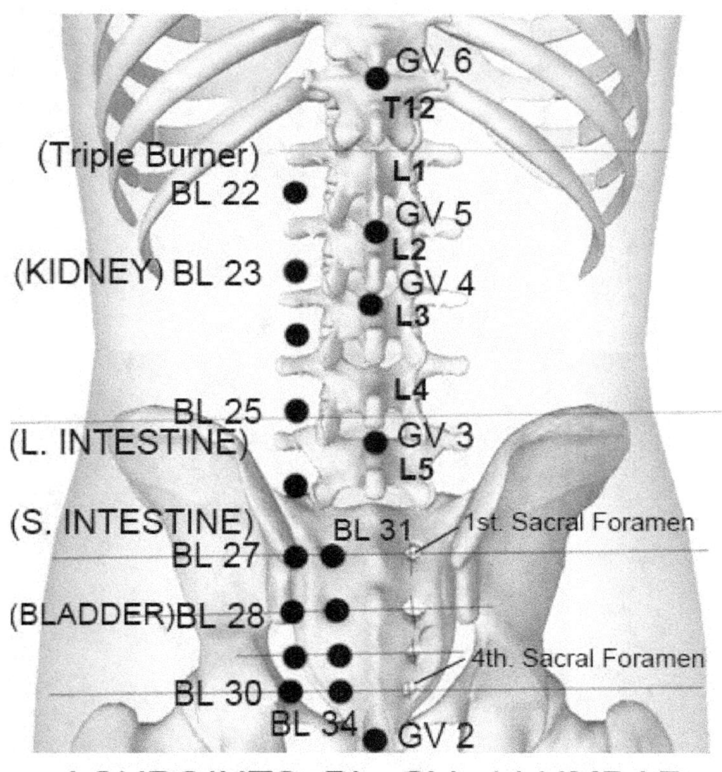

ACUPOINTS: BL, GV at LUMBAR

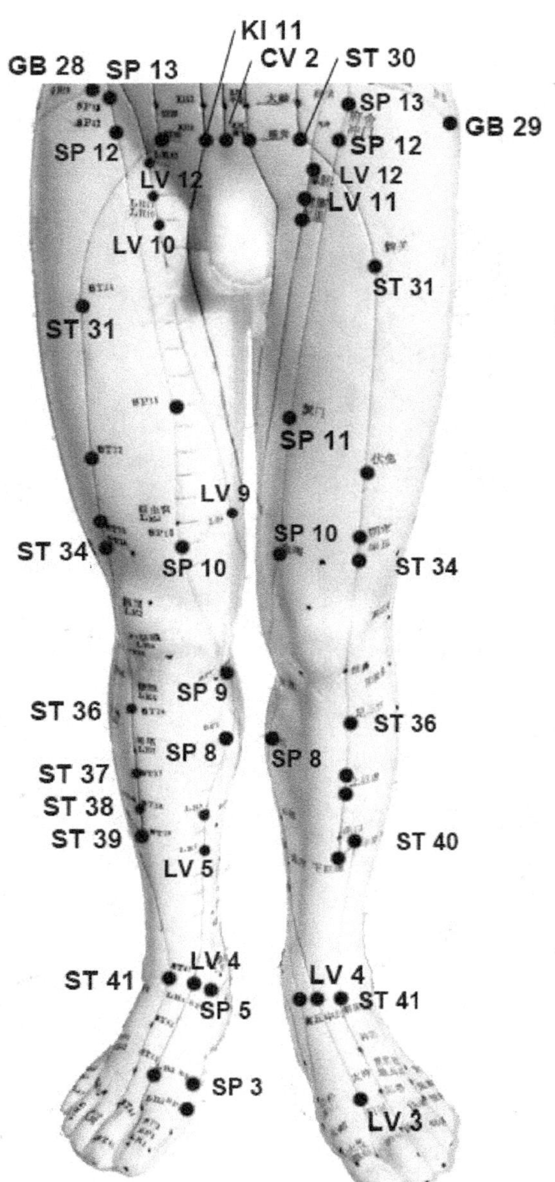

ACUPOINTS: FRONT OF LEG

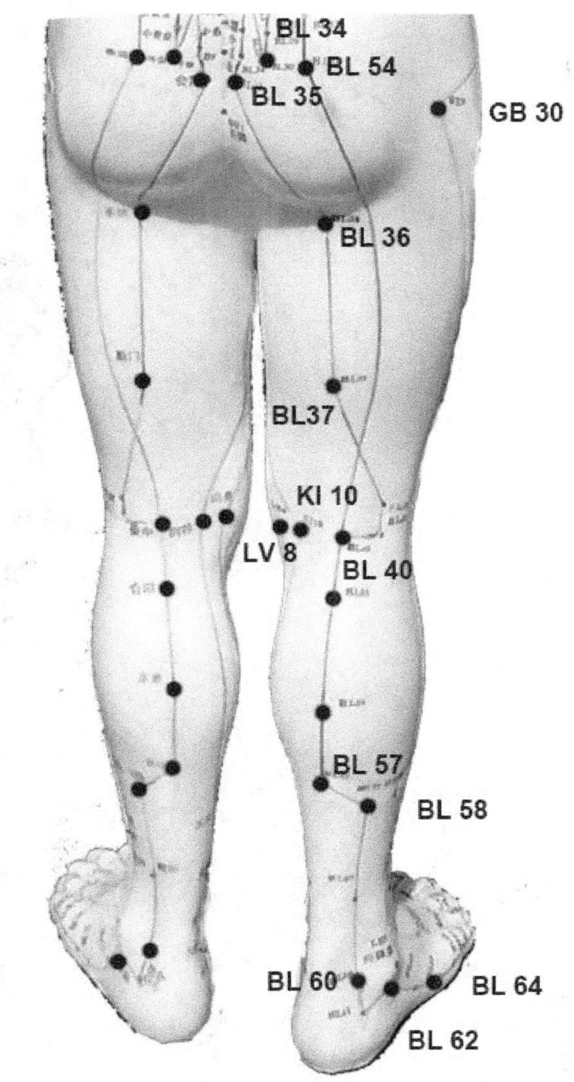

ACUPOINTS: BEHIND THE LEG

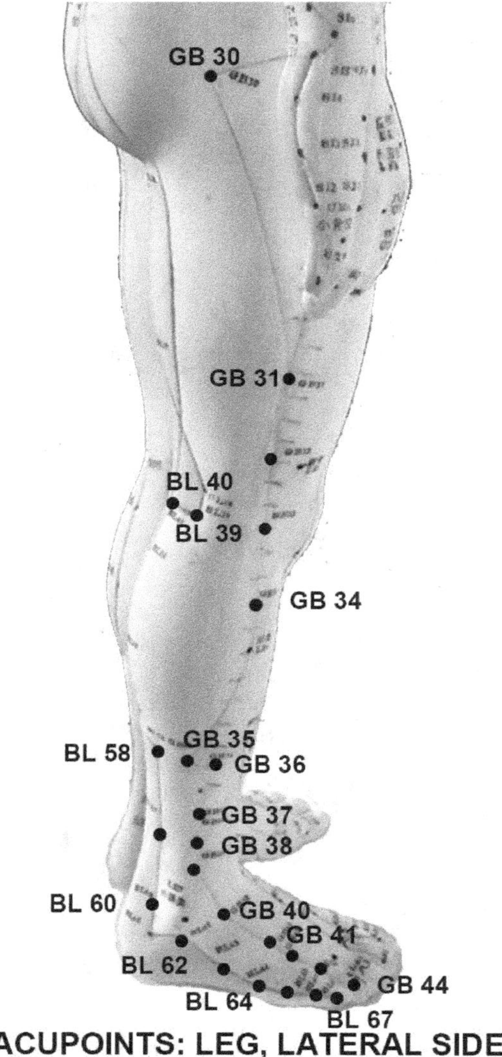

ACUPOINTS: LEG, LATERAL SIDE

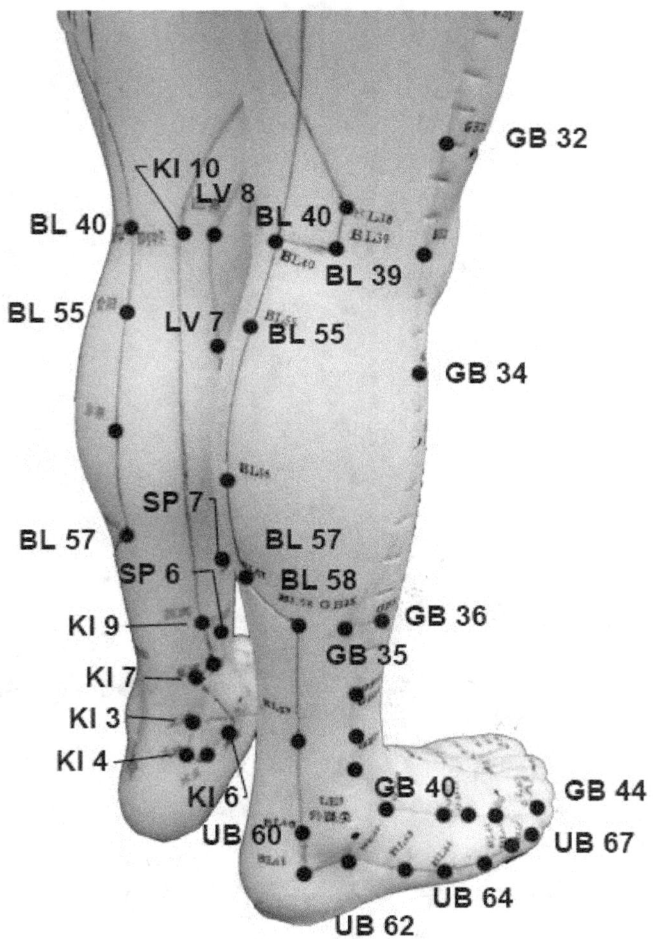

ACUPOINTS : LEG, BEHIND

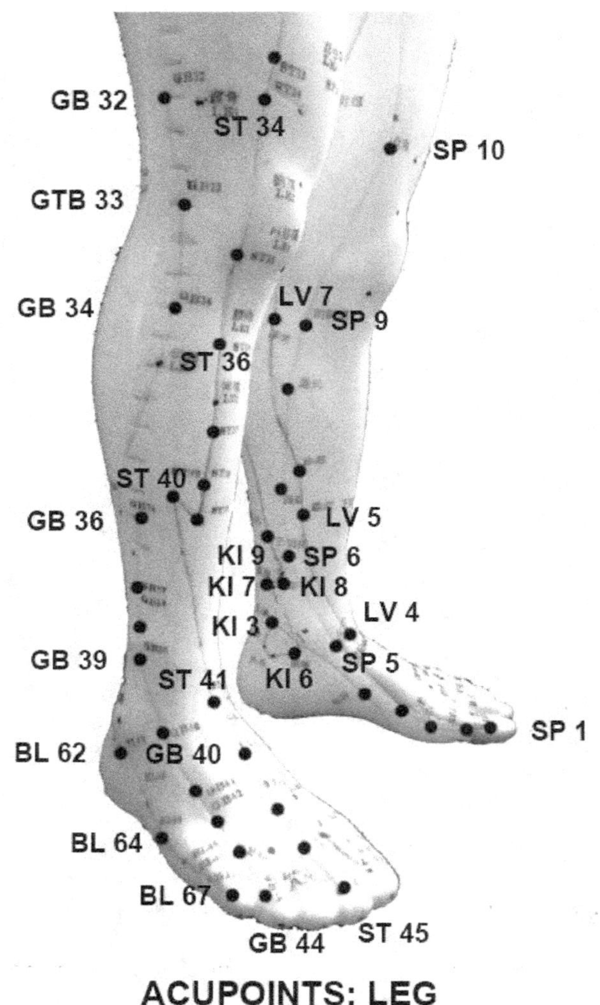

ACUPOINTS: LEG

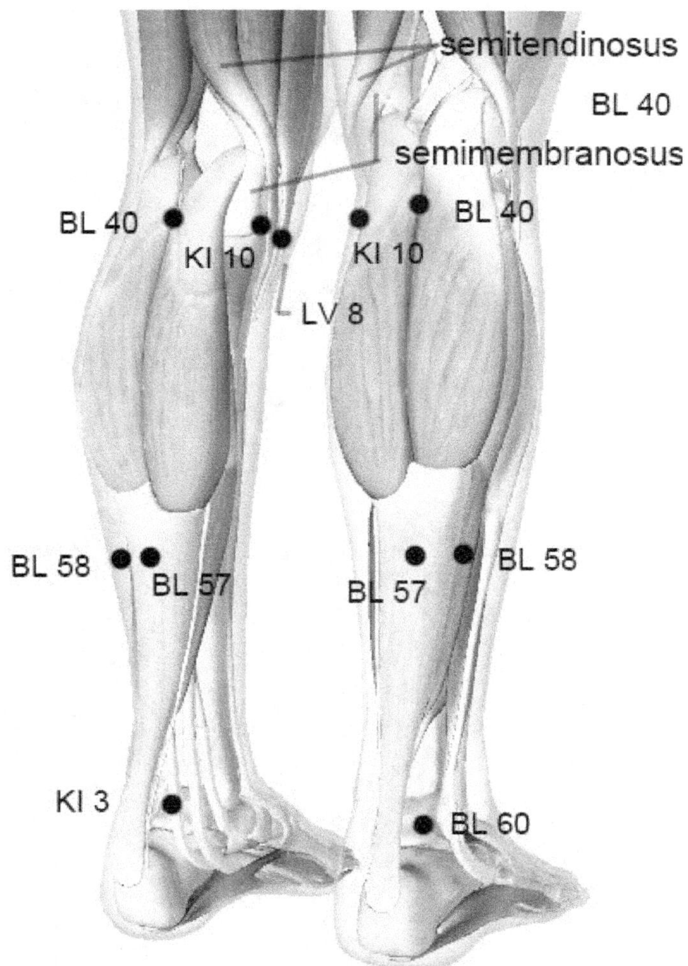

ACUPOINTS: LEG, BEHIND

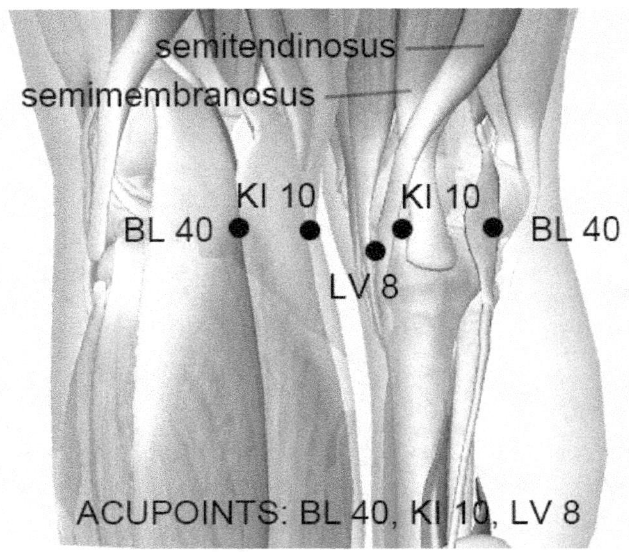

semitendinosus
semimembranosus
KI 10
KI 10
BL 40
LV 8
BL 40
ACUPOINTS: BL 40, KI 10, LV 8

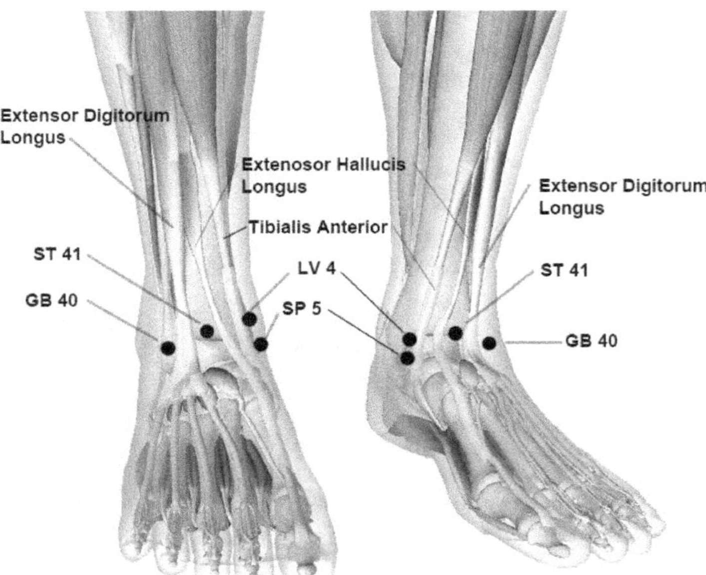

Extensor Digitorum Longus
Extenosor Hallucis Longus
Tibialis Anterior
Extensor Digitorum Longus
ST 41
LV 4
ST 41
GB 40
SP 5
GB 40
ACUPOINTS: GB 40, SP 5, LV 4, ST 41

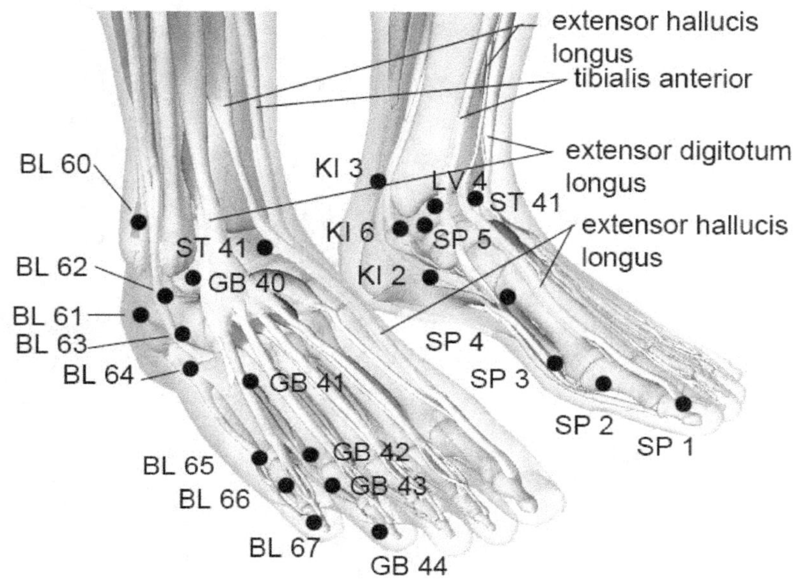

ACUPOINTS: FOOT

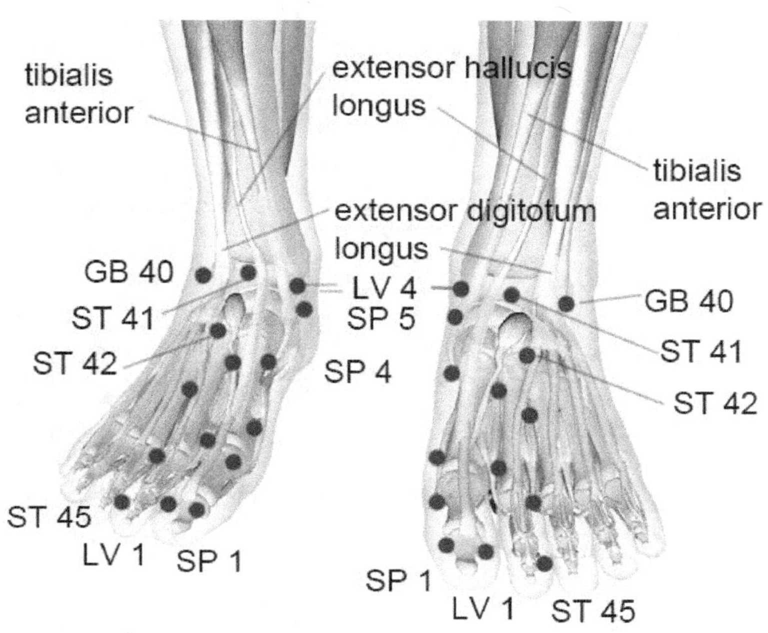

ACUPOINTS: FOOT TOP, SP, LV, ST

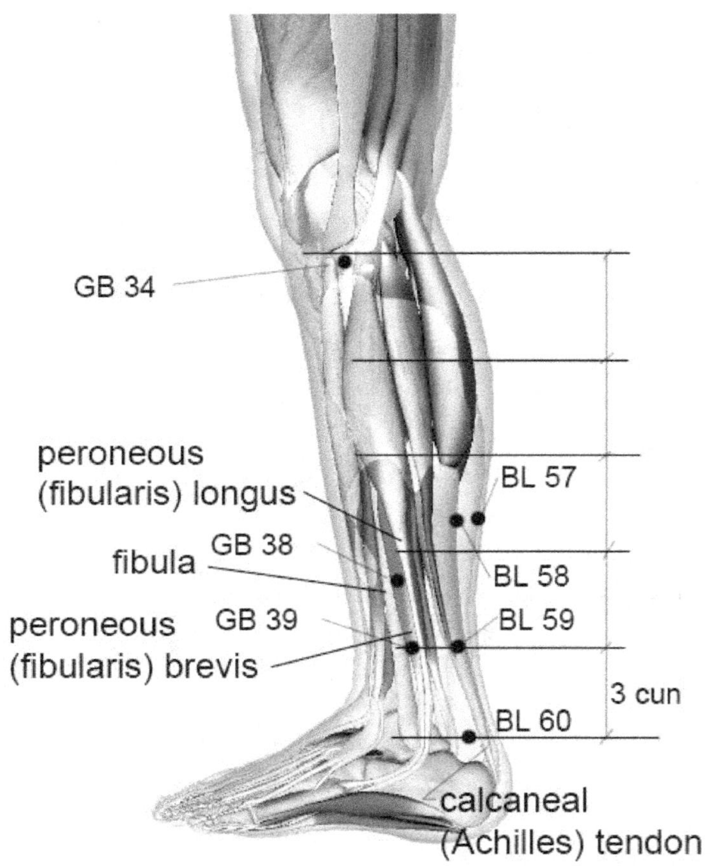

ACUPOINTS: LEG, SIDE

EPILOGUE

I hope information in this book is helpful to understand pain and how to treat it using magnets on acupuncture points. It is the most simple and easiest way to help oneself with life limiting minor aches and pains that people are dealing with in normal daily life. If you have serious health problem, you should consultant with healthcare professionals. However, acupoint magnet therapy is something you can do yourself when nothing seems to help. Do not try to treat undiagnosed health problems by yourself.

Please send your comments and questions to
namjeon@sprynet.com   Web: www.namjeon.com

Nam W. Jeon, AP, L.Ac.   October 1, 2019

ABOUT THE AUTHOR

Nam W. Jeon, AP, L.Ac.

Nam is licensed in the State of Florida and certified by NCCAOM (the National Certification Commission of Acupuncture and Oriental Medicine).

He graduated from the Midwest College of Oriental Medicine, Chicago, IL. with Masters of Science in Oriental Medicine. He has advanced training from Guangzhou Hospital in China and has been working for wellness centers and private practice for twenty years in the Midwest and in Fairbanks, Alaska before settling in Lakeland, FL, in 2016.

Nam uses his knowledge and experience in acupuncture and Chinese herbs to treat the person as a whole, focusing not only on the symptom but also the root cause of the problem.

He has been effectively treating patients with complaints ranging from musculoskeletal pain (low back pain, sciatica, tennis elbow, bursitis, arthritis) and neurological disorders (insomnia, headaches, migraines). He also specialized in treating emotional disorders (stress, anxiety, depression), addictions (drug, alcohol, nicotine). He sincerely listens to the patient's needs and difficulties, and tries to find the way to resolve problems beyond acupuncture and herbs. He also teaches stress management and mindful meditation.

He has been writing books and travel blogs in his leisure time. Here are links you can checkout his work.

Here are links where you can find his eBooks;
https://www.amazon.com/s/ref=nb_sb_noss?url=node%3D154606011&field-keywords=nam+jeon

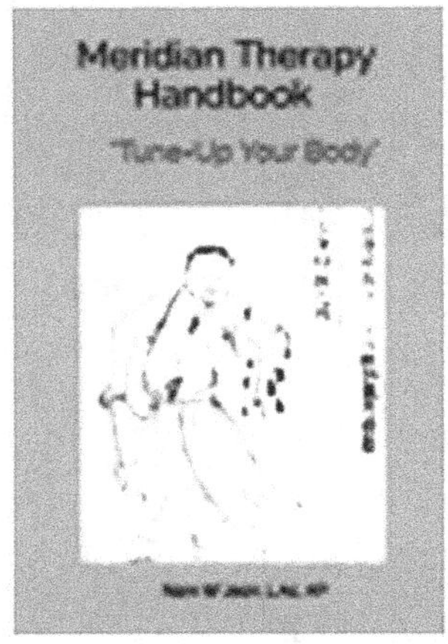

"Meridian Therapy Handbook: Tune-Up your Body"

Introduction of the Five Phase Acupuncture (Sa Ahm Acupuncture).

The Ancient Healer"
Introduction of the theoretical back ground of the Oriental Medicine.

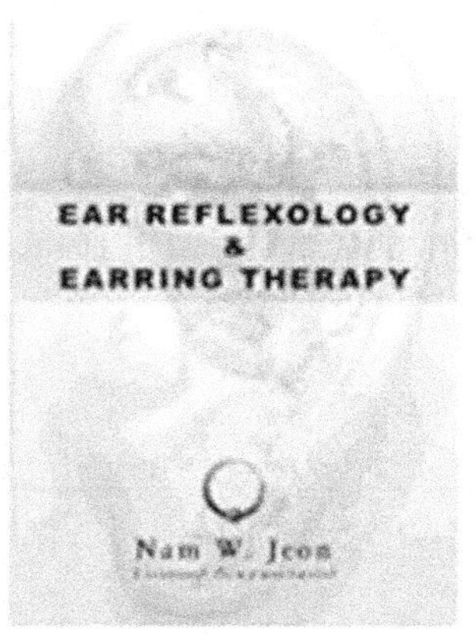

"Ear Reflexology & Earring Therapy"
Introduces ear reflexology to treat pain and functional disorders. He has lecture series on pain treatment by ear acupuncture in YouTube.

" BioMedicine Essential: BioMedicine Study Guide for the Oriental Medicine Practitioner"

Study guide for acupuncture students who prepare for the board license exam.

"Cruising around the Europe"
A travel blog that he wrote while he was working on a cruise ship.